MW01234626

Printed in the United State of America

First paperback edition October 2019

ISBN 978-0-578-50917-4

Published by Old Dog Publishing LLC

The
Senior Dog
FOREVER IN MY HEART

The
Senior Dog
FOREVER IN MY HEART

Introduction

Your best friend has gotten older.

However, that's not what you see when you look at her.

No, when you look into that furry face, you don't see the grey that now coats her muzzle. You don't see the cataracts in her eyes, or at least you pretend you don't. You try not to worry about the short, wheezing breaths or the concerned looks that she gives you whenever you get up, almost as if she's afraid you will leave the room and not come back.

You don't get upset when it takes her longer to get up out of her bed and when she sometimes seems confused about what door takes her outside. The accidents she has don't bother you because you love her. She's provided you with so much love and affection over the years that there's nothing she could do, no mess she could make, that would ever make you think less of her.

When you look at her, you still see that adorable little face that you've known for so long. You still see the silly little puppy that you loved so much when you brought her home… only to realize that your love was capable of continuing to grow and become stronger in the intervening years.

You've spent a lot of time together.

But that's still not enough.

She's older now, and even though you don't want to see it, you know it. You know that times are changing and that her needs are changing. You know that your time together, as painful as it is to hear, is limited.

She's in her twilight days, and you want to do absolutely everything you can to make sure that she is as healthy, happy, and comfortable as possible.

Anyone who has been fortunate enough to be a part of a dog's life knows these feelings. It's not a pleasant time, but you need to continue to be strong if you hope to make those last months and days as comfortable as possible.

This books is dedicated to helping you learn more about caring for the senior dog in your life and making sure that she is able to remain as healthy and happy as possible for as long as possible. It's not easy, but your best friend is well worth it.

Chapter 1: About Your Dog

We've all heard people say that every year of a dog's life is equivalent to seven human years. Many of you might even have believed that statement and sworn by it when you were trying to determine just how old your dog would be considered if they were human. However, as popular as that idea might be, it's not true at all.

Dogs Age Differently

What is true is that dogs will age differently, and much faster, than people. Yet, not all dogs will age at the same rate. It is very dependent upon the size of the dog, as you can see from the list below. Check out the list to get a better understanding of just how old your dog truly is. Also, keep in mind that this is not an exact science, and the ages are the best approximations possible.

Small Dogs (20lbs or less)

- Year 1 = Age 15 human years
- Year 2 = Age 24 human years
- Year 3 = Age 28 human years
- Year 4 = Age 32 human years
- Year 5 = Age 36 human years
- Year 6 = Age 40 human years
- Year 7 = Age 44 human years
- Year 8 = Age 48 human years
- Year 9 = Age 52 human years
- Year 10 = Age 56 human years
- Year 11 = Age 60 human years
- Year 12 = Age 64 human years
- Year 13 = Age 68 human years
- Year 14 = Age 72 human years
- Year 15 = Age 76 human years
- Year 16 = Age 80 human years

Medium Dogs (21lbs to 50lbs)

- Year 1 = Age 15 human years
- Year 2 = Age 24 human years
- Year 3 = Age 28 human years
- Year 4 = Age 32 human years
- Year 5 = Age 36 human years
- Year 6 = Age 42 human years
- Year 7 = Age 47 human years
- Year 8 = Age 51 human years
- Year 9 = Age 56 human years
- Year 10 = Age 60 human years
- Year 11 = Age 65 human years
- Year 12 = Age 69 human years
- Year 13 = Age 74 human years
- Year 14 = Age 78 human years
- Year 15 = Age 83 human years
- Year 16 = Age 87 human years

Large Dogs (51lbs and up)

- Year 1 = Age 15 human years
- Year 2 = Age 24 human years
- Year 3 = Age 28 human years
- Year 4 = Age 32 human years
- Year 5 = Age 36 human years
- Year 6 = Age 45 human years
- Year 7 = Age 50 human years
- Year 8 = Age 55 human years
- Year 9 = Age 61 human years
- Year 10 = Age 66 human years
- Year 11 = Age 72 human years
- Year 12 = Age 77 human years

- Year 13 = Age 82 human years
- Year 14 = Age 88 human years
- Year 15 = Age 93 human years
- Year 16 = Age 120 human years

You can see that it's quite a bit different than the seven years that is typically associated with determining the human age equivalent of dogs. The handy chart above can help to give you a better idea of the true age of your dog. Again, you will want to keep in mind that this is an *approximation* of their age.

Signs of Aging

As the dogs get older, they will often show certain signs that they are aging, but it can be somewhat different with each dog. Some of the typical signs of aging will include gray fur that forms initially around the muzzle and then spreads to other areas of the face, the head, and the body. The dog might also have teeth that are starting to show more signs of wear and tear. They could have cloudy eyes and trouble moving around, as well. In the case of some dogs, they might have trouble holding their bladders or bowels until they are able to make it outside.

While there are certainly differences in the way that dogs age compared with humans, at least in terms of how long it takes, the symptoms and signs mentioned above do have quite a few similarities, as well.

As with humans, when a dog gets older, they face more challenges and different types of challenges than when they were young and spry.

Let's take some time to get a better understanding of what some of these challenges are and things that you, as a loving friend to your canine companion, can do to help make things a bit better and easier for them.

Aging Challenges

Different dogs will age differently from one another, as well. Even if you have two small chihuahuas who grew up together, or are even siblings, they may face different challenges as they get older. Therefore, it is important that you take some time to understand some of the most common aging challenges that canines face and how you can help them.

By having better knowledge of what your dog is going through, you can find more ways to ease them during any issues they might be having in their old age. After all, they have always been there for you, so now it is time for you to make sure you are there for them.

After discussing the basics of these challenges, we will be discussing some different types of supplies that you can use to help meet and handle those challenges.

Eating and Drinking

In some cases, you will find that your elderly dog is not eating and drinking the same way they did when they were a pup. Having an understanding of why they might not be eating and drinking, or why they might be eating and drinking too much, can give you some more insight into what could be wrong.

Issues with eating and drinking, whether they indulge too much or not enough, is a concern. Whenever there is *any* doubt, make an appointment with the vet. One of the themes that you will see throughout this book is that it is always better to be safe rather than sorry.

Not Enough Water

There are many reasons that the dog might not seem to be drinking enough water. In some cases, older dogs might not be going to the water dish as much because it requires a lot of effort on their part. This could be the case with dogs that are quite old and who have trouble getting around.

If you believe this to be the case, you have a couple of options here. You could find ways to make it easier for the dog to get to the water or you could bring the water to the dog. You might also want to mix the dog food with water. If the dog is eating normally, and they are just not drinking, this could be a good way to get some extra hydration into them. However, you will typically want to speak with your veterinarian before you change the dog's food.

Of course, there are other reasons that the dog might not be drinking enough water, as well. Illness could be a factor, and even a change in their surroundings or in their life could cause them to become less inclined to drink. In some cases, it might just be nervousness about new surroundings, for example, and they will eventually settle down and then eat or drink normally.

If you notice that your dog still is not drinking regardless of what you've tried, it is time to get in touch with the vet.

Too Much Water

If the dog happens to be drinking an excessive amount of water, particularly an elderly dog, it could be a sign of a medical problem. Some of the most common medical problems that could cause dogs to drink extra water include kidney failure, diabetes, and Cushing's disease.

We will talk more about these types of diseases and problems with dogs later in the book. In addition, there are certain medications that a dog might be taking, such as prednisone, which will cause them to need to drink more water. If you believe that your dog is drinking more water than they should be, you will want to speak with the vet sooner rather than later.

Not Eating Enough

Sometimes, elderly dogs that used to have a big appetite stop eating like they once did. When you have a dog that used to always want treats and that used to look at the food bowl longingly before it was time for their dinner suddenly stop caring about food, it can be quite alarming.

There could be many different reasons that they are no longer eating as much as they once did. Again, it could be because of illness or disease, which your vet should be able to catch and provide some guidance for you. The changes in appetite can also be because they have problems with their teeth. Just like humans, teeth can become sore, loose, and cavities can develop. If the teeth hurt, they are less likely to want to eat, even if they are hungry.

With elderly dogs, problematic teeth are more common. However, you cannot simply assume this is the case. Once again, your best and safest course of action is to speak with a veterinarian, as there could be other medical reasons that the dog is not eating. The sooner you know the true cause and what to do about it the better.

Poor nutrition can lead to a number of problems in your dog. These include:
- Weakness and lethargy
- Loss of muscle tissue
- Inability to metabolize medications that are being taken for other health issues

- A slower healing capability, which can be particularly problematic if the dog is dealing with other illnesses or diseases

It is also important to keep in mind that if a dog is not eating regularly, it will make them a poor candidate for surgery. If they need surgery to help them deal with another type of issue they are suffering, this can become very problematic.

There are many different methods that you can try to attempt to get the dog to eat more. You could change the type of food, as long as it is still healthy for them, to see if they like something else better. You could switch to a soft food if you think it might be a problem with their teeth. You could add some water to their dry food. Try a few different methods to see if you can find one that works well for your dog and that helps to stimulate the appetite.

Eating Too Much

This tends to be much less of a problem when it comes to elderly dogs. Most of the time, people have trouble getting their older and sometimes more finicky dogs to eat. If the problem is that your senior dog is eating too much, it can also be a health problem.

In some cases, medications can cause an increase in hunger in the dog. Internal parasites could cause increased hunger, as well, and these can occur in dogs of all ages.

Various types of medical conditions can cause increases in hunger, too. Hormonal imbalances, cancer, diabetes, and problems with the intestines or the pancreas could be to blame. These are issues that you won't be able to diagnose on your own, so once again, it is time to head to the vet with your beloved dog.

Changes in appetite and the desire to drink are often indicators that something is wrong with the animal. When the dog is not eating or drinking normally, it is important that you continue to watch for other signs and symptoms. For example, do they have problems with vomiting and/or diarrhea? Do they have issues with incontinence? We will look closer at these issues in the upcoming parts of this chapter.

The more information you have available regarding the condition and symptoms of your dog the better it will be for the vet, as it can help them to determine what might be wrong and what they can do to help.

Elimination/Incontinence Problems

Older dogs can also have problems with elimination and incontinence. In some cases, the dogs might be suffering from canine cognitive dysfunction, which will be discussed in detail later in the book. This problem can sometimes lead dogs to being confused, not knowing where they are, and not knowing or remembering that they should be outside when they do their business.

Of course, there are also a number of other problems that could be causing the dog to soil the home. Sensory decline, as well as neuromuscular conditions can affect a dog greatly. In the case of the neuromuscular conditions, it can be difficult or even impossible for the dog to get up and go out to relieve themselves.

The dog could also be suffering from other issues, such as endocrine system disorders, brain tumors, and other disorders that could increase the frequency of elimination. Issues that *decrease the control* the dog has over their bladder or bowel could cause elimination and incontinence issues in the home as well.

Some of the other common medical issues that could cause the dogs to soil the home include:

- Bladder infections
- Kidney stones
- Diabetes
- Cushing's disease
- Intestinal parasites

- Pancreatic problems
- Gastroenteritis

Of course, these are just some of the potential medical issues that the dog might be suffering. Your veterinarian will be able to narrow down the problem further to provide a diagnosis and a course of treatment.

There is also the possibility that the dog could be suffering from separation anxiety. While this is most common in puppies and dogs who are new to the home, it can also occur with elderly dogs who become worried when their human companions are not around them. This separation anxiety and nervousness can result in the dog having accidents around the house. Along the same lines, if there are changes to the environment in the home of an older dog, or a change in their schedule, anxiety can develop as well.

First, of course, you will want to check with the veterinarian to see whether it is a health problem physically or if the issues are identified as anxiety. Once you determine the crux of the problem, it will become somewhat easier to handle or at least easier to understand.

Vomiting and Diarrhea

Many older dogs also suffer from vomiting and diarrhea on a regular basis, and the reasons for this can vary just as widely as the other problems discussed in this chapter. Naturally, this is unpleasant for both you and your dog. In some instances, it might not be serious – it might just mean that Fido has been getting into the trash.

However, if you have an older dog who is consistently vomiting and/or who consistently has diarrhea, the problem could be far more serious. In some cases it could be Addison's disease. This disease occurs when the endocrine system inside the dog does not produce the hormones needed for their body to function properly.

If your dog does suffer from Addison's disease, some of the symptoms that they may show include:

- Lethargy
- Muscle weakness
- Low body temperature
- Reduced heart rate

Of course, the dog could be suffering from vomiting and diarrhea for other reasons, as well. Intestinal worms and other types of parasites could be the cause of the problem. Upper urinary tract infections and kidney disease could cause a problem resulting in vomiting and diarrhea, as well. The dog might also suffer from hypothyroidism. If this is the case, they will exhibit different types of signs. These include:

- Weight gain
- Fur loss
- Lethargy
- Frequent ear infections
- Thickened skin, which might be noticeable around the folds of the eyes
- Dull coat

If your dog has problems with vomiting and diarrhea, you need to get to the veterinarian to have it handled professionally.

Hygiene

Let's be honest, even in the best of days, the hygiene of dogs is not always as good as you might like. They might get into the trash, the toilet, and a host of other messes that can cause their breath and their coat to get a little stinky. They are dogs; they do weird things, and they really are not aware of their own hygiene. A dog does not care if it has bad breath.

However, you do. With proper care and bathing, it is possible to help improve the hygiene of the dog, making their teeth strong, their breath good, and their coat shiny. Typically, that's all you need for younger dogs.

Of course, as the dog gets older, their hygiene can suffer in ways that are not quite as easily remedied. Older dogs who have extremely stinky breath could have that condition because they are suffering from periodontal disease.

If you have a dog who is suffering from periodontal disease, you want to consult with your veterinarian to determine the best way to treat it. If periodontal disease is left unchecked, it can cause a host of other issues for your dog. If the teeth are loose, in pain, or they fall out, naturally, it will be difficult for the dog to eat. As we've mentioned, this will result in other health issues.

In addition, you want to keep in mind that periodontal disease really will affect more than just the teeth. The bacteria in the mouth secrete toxins and these toxins can cause damage to the heart tissue, the brain tissue, and the kidneys. Bad breath could mean there are other more serious issues that could be coming in the future.

There are veterinary dentistry procedures that can help with periodontitis. Of course, since the majority of dogs who suffer from this problem tend to be older, their owners are concerned about the safety of their dog undergoing those dental procedures. Fortunately, most otherwise healthy, senior dogs will be able to undergo the procedures without suffering an undue amount of risk.

Prevention tends to be the best option, so if your dog's currently suffering from dental issues, you will want to work on taking better care of their teeth now. This can help problems from developing later.

There are toothbrushes specifically for dogs, flavored toothpastes the dogs can enjoy, and even antiseptic impregnated treats that can help with their teeth. Make sure your dentist is looking at the teeth whenever your dog has a checkup, regardless of the dog's age, as well.

Sleeping

While most dogs do not have a problem sleeping, that certainly is not always the case, especially with older dogs. This can occur for a range of reasons, including cognitive dysfunction. This can cause them to wake up and vocalize during the middle of the night.

With older dogs, the hearing and eyesight could also be weakened and this could cause some to have a fear of the dark. This can make it more difficult for them to get to sleep, and again, could cause them to bark in the middle of the night.

In addition, there are certain medications, such as prednisone, that can cause insomnia in dogs. Illness, aches and pains, and other symptoms of aging can also cause the dog to wake up more easily.

It is important to keep in mind that not being able to sleep is only one of the potential sleeping problems that older dogs might have. In some cases, you may find that your older dog sleeps a lot. In fact, you might think they are sleeping too much. Keep in mind that older dogs do sleep more than younger dogs; just like elderly people tend to sleep more than younger people. It is the nature of time and how it wears on the body.

However, there are certainly some medical conditions that can cause dogs to sleep too much.

Many veterinarians believe that it is possible for dogs to become depressed, again just as humans do. When they go through changes in their life or living situation, or pretty much anything in their routine, it can create a chemical imbalance in the brain. This can result in depression. Dogs suffering from hypothyroidism, diabetes, and certain infectious diseases could sleep far more than other dogs, as well.

Sometimes, an older dog can sleep up to 20 hours a day and it won't be a problem. It will all depend on what is causing the dog to sleep so much. Those who are concerned that their dog may be spending too much time sleeping should get in touch with the veterinarian.

Walking

Most dogs love to get out and go for walks. They like to run and play. That's even true with many older dogs. However, some dogs into their senior years simply aren't able to do as much for a range of reasons. They are not as strong as they once were, they might be suffering from disease or other illnesses, and they may not have the motivation to get out and walk as much.

However, it is still important to attempt to take the dog out for a walk. You need to understand the dog' s limits in their older age, however. This means that you won't be able to go on those long walks and hikes with them. It means they probably aren't going to be running and jumping like they used to. Therefore, you want to create an exercise routine that will work for the dog's current condition.

A range of conditions could limit mobility in older dogs. One of the most common and chronic issues seen in dogs that will limit their mobility is osteoarthritis. This is a degeneration of the joints that typically happens naturally over time, which is why it tends to affect older dogs. It can also be a problem with dogs that are overweight, as they have more wear and tear on the joints.

Other issues that can crop up include hip dysplasia, which is common in breeds such as German Shepherds. Rheumatoid arthritis, as well as infections such as Lyme disease, could also limit mobility. Older dogs could also be suffering from other injuries that were incurred during slipping or sliding into something. Just as with people, things don't "bounce back" quite like they once did.

This means the exercise tolerance may be lower. Just because you can't go out for the long walks you did before, there are still other things you can do. Going on shorter walks, playing around the house, and swimming can be excellent activities that will help to exercise the body without putting too much pain on the joints. Limit the amount of time spent on the activities and make sure they get enough rest and hydration.

Taking Medications

Dogs of all ages tend to have problems taking their medications. However, as a dog gets older, they need to have quite a few more of these meds to help them remain healthier for longer. Therefore, it is helpful to have a few tricks up your sleeve to help your dog get these meds into their system ... even if they hate taking their meds.

Supplies for Helping with Aging Challenges

As you have seen, quite a few aging challenges affect senior dogs. You want to make sure you are doing everything you can to keep your dog as happy and healthy as possible. This means you need to consider some of the different ways that you can help with those aging challenges.

Below, you will find some tips and supplies that can be used to help with a range of the aging issues that we've mentioned, as well as some new ones.

For Elimination Problems

If your dog suffers from elimination and incontinence problems, you might feel like you're at your wits end. Let's look at a few of the things you can do to help make the problem a little bit more bearable for everyone. This will not provide you with a cure for the problem, but it will make things easier to care for in the home.

Move the Dog's Bed

Have you thought that currently the dog's bed might be a little too far from the door? If your dog still has enough awareness to realize that they have to go to the bathroom, but they are unable to get outside fast enough, it could be because they can't get to the door to let you know.

By moving the dog bed a bit closer to the door, it reduces the distance they have to travel. However, you do want to make sure that the dog does not feel as though they are being separated from the rest of the family when you do this. Always weigh the pros and cons before you move the bed. In addition, if you are going to move the bed, you will want to be sure that you do not place it in an area that is drafty.

Keep the Bed Safe from Fluids

If your dog has accidents, you should make it a point to take some precautions and protect items that could become wet or soiled. The bed, which is where the dog tends to spend a lot of time is an area you will certainly want to protect from getting soiled.

A good and simple method of protecting the dog's bed is to get a plastic cover for it. Your dog is not going to want to sleep on top of plastic, of course, so you also need to have a small blanket – that you don't care if it gets ruined – that you can place on top of the plastic.

Ideally, you want a plastic that is not going to make too much noise when the dog shifts their weight and tries to settle down onto the bed. The sound could make some dogs nervous.

When an accident does occur, you will wash the towel or blanket and hose off the plastic cover and let it dry before replacing it. Of course, for those who have the money to spend, there are also waterproof dog beds. These beds are made specifically to withstand accidents. They could be a good investment for those older dogs that have been having some problems with incontinence and elimination.

A number of companies are making these types of dog beds today, including PetFusion and Milliard. However, before you choose *any* dog bed for your dog, you will want to check out the information that follows, in order give you some tips on how to be sure you are picking out the *right* dog bed for your furry best friend.

Consider Adding a Doggie Door

Another option that you may want to consider using is adding a doggie door to the backdoor, or the front door if you have a fenced yard that the dog will not be able to wander away from when they go out unsupervised.

While not everyone will want to have one of these types of doors in their home, they can make it much easier for the dogs if they need to go out and relieve themselves. It's a way for them to make a fast exit.

There are many of these types of doggie doors on the market today that can be installed onto doors, and even into walls in some cases. While these have the potential to be helpful, and they can work for some homes, they may not always be the best solution. This is because you have to think about the fact that other animals could also get inside your house – even animals you don't want in there. You really don't need a raccoon coming in and making itself at home. The same is true of any other animal.

You also have to think about the weather in your area. If you live in a location where it tends to be cold, you may not want a dog running in and out and letting the cold air inside. It also allows for drafts to come inside. Of course, there are some high-tech doggie doors that can help to eliminate some of these issues. If you are going to get one of these doors, you want to be sure it will meet your home's needs.

Dog Incontinence Diapers

To be honest, this is going to be something your dog probably won't like. Wearing incontinence diapers for a dog is going to feel strange and it will take them time to adjust. An exception to this rule might be those dogs that have been accustomed to wearing sweaters and other getups throughout their life.

Still, these diapers, which are very similar to human diapers except that they have a hole for a tail, can be a good solution for dogs that are having some serious problems with their bowels or bladder control.

You can find a range of different types and brands of these dog diapers on the market today, including those that are disposable and those that are washable.

Pee Pads

You might have used these pads when your dog was just a puppy. They are absorbent paper that are often used to help puppies become potty-trained. However, now that the dog is older and is suffering from incontinence issues, they could be a very good option to place in certain areas around the house, as well. It will help to make cleanup quite a bit easier.

These are a simple and beneficial option because they tend to be quite easy to use and they are priced reasonably. Again, there are a number of brands and styles of these on the market today. You can even find those that have artificial or real grass, which may be a better option for certain dogs.

Pet Odor Remover and Cleaners

Even when you take the precautions mentioned here and use the supplies mentioned, it doesn't mean you're able to catch every accident. There will still be accidents that your senior dog cannot help. Therefore, having a quality pet odor remover on hand will help you to make sure your home does not stink terribly.

Some of the different brands that are available today include:
- Rocco & Roxie
- Sunny & Honey
- OdoBan
- Angry Orange
- Nature's Miracle
- Bissell Woolite

Of course these are just some of the options. Naturally, you will want to research the options that are available and find the one that has the scent that you prefer – or no scent for that matter – and that works well for your needs. The same is true of the cleaning products that you choose to help deal with stains.

Use a Black Light

How do you know you're getting all the urine when you're cleaning up? Even if you think you do a good job with the cleaning, you might not be.

If you want to be sure that you're getting the area as clean as possible, consider using a black light. When you use this type of light, the urine will glow in the dark under the illumination, letting you know where you still need to clean. This makes sure that your area is entirely clean, and it will also help with the odor control mentioned earlier.

For Eating and Drinking Problems

We touched on this earlier in the book. When your dog is having issues with eating and drinking, it can be difficult to get them to get the nutrients and the hydration they need. However, there are some tips and some supplies that will help you along the way.

For Mobility Problems

Many dogs who are older suffer from mobility problems, as mentioned. This means it tends to be quite difficult for them to get around as easily as they once did. Fortunately, there are things that you can do as a means to help things become at least a little bit easier for them.

It tends to be very difficult for dogs who are elderly or in pain to get up and move around when they're on a slick floor surface. You will not have to replace all the flooring in your home, of course. You can find some very effective options that you can use to make it a little easier for your dog to get around the house.

Nonslip Area Rugs and Runners

You don't need to cover your entire house with these, but you will want to put them in the areas where the dog tends to spend a lot of time. They will make it easier for the dog to cross hardwood floors, tile floors, and linoleum floors. These types of surfaces might be too slick for them otherwise. Even if they *could* walk across them, they might not have the confidence that they did when they were younger. They could cause slip and fall injuries for the dog that could create even more health issues.

Nonslip Stair Treads to Hardwood Staircases

Along the same lines, if you have hardwood staircases that the dog used to be able to go up and down with no problem when they were younger, that is not likely to be the case now that they are old.

Therefore, you should consider getting some treads or bits of carpeting that you can add to the staircases. These will make it much easier for the dog to go up and down the stairs. However, as the dog continues to get older, the trip up and down the stairs will continue become more and more difficult. At some point, the dog might be relegated to staying downstairs entirely unless you have another safe means of conveying them between the floors regularly.

Gripping Booties

You might still have some areas of the home that are difficult for the dog to walk through, or they might be heading out with you to the vet, to the pet store to pick up some food and a toy or visiting friends and family. You can't expect everywhere you go to cater to your dog, so you need to find ways that will help to make their mobility a bit easier.

Gripping booties that they can wear like socks or shoes could be a good option for you to consider. As with the diapers, these might not be a product that your dog takes to right away. It can take some time for them to get accustomed to using them. Start out slowly and use praise and treats with them, just as you did when you were training your dog as a puppy.

It will take some time in many cases, but you can often get the dog accustomed to wearing them, and it can help them from sliding and slipping when they are moving around.

Ramp for the Vehicle and/or the Bed

If you take your dog with you when you go places, you might have noticed that they have more and more difficult getting into and out of the vehicle. They used to be able to hop up easily and now, they just stand there and look at the interior of the vehicle gauging whether they think they can make the leap ... it's sad to see.

When you have a simple little portable ramp or step, it will give the dog an easy way to get into and out of the vehicle. You can also use these ramps and steps in the home if your dog is accustomed to sleeping up on the bed or hanging out on the sofa. It helps to reduce the risk of injury as they are getting up and down.

Doggie Wheelchair

If your dog has severe mobility problems, but they still need to get out and about, you might want to consider a doggie wheelchair. While these can be expensive, they can help to ensure that your dog can still get out and go for walks and have at least some semblance of a better quality of life as they are getting older.

These wheelchairs are a good option for those who are looking to provide some additional stability for their canine companions. It will help to provide the dog with more confidence, and it can let them remain more self-sufficient.

As with other products mentioned here, these can take some getting used to by your dog. Work at it daily and give it some time. They will come around, and it will help to return to them some of the mobility that they used to enjoy.

For Dogs Who Wander (Tracking Tools)

If you have an elderly dog that gets out of the house and takes off, wandering to who knows where, you know just how scary this can be. You want them to be safe, but you are never sure if they are going to make it home this time.

Fortunately, technology has caught up to this problem, and there are tracking tools and devices that can be used with your dog, whether they are elderly or not, that will help you quickly and easily track them down.

You can find collar attachments that can attach quickly and easily, and that will let you track down your pet right from an app on your smartphone.

Even though the best quality trackers tend to be on the expensive side, if you have a dog that wanders a lot, you will want to consider getting one of these trackers. There are a number of brands and models available from companies like Findster and Tractive.

Always take the time to check out some reviews to get a better idea of the actual quality of the trackers you are considering, and to see whether the tracker has the features that you need.

How to Choose a Dog Bed

You want to be sure that your senior dog has a nice bed where they will feel comfortable when they are resting. Not just any dog bed will do. You really do need to take the time to make sure that you are getting the right bed for your dog's needs and ailments. Let's look at what you will need to consider when it comes to choosing the ideal dog bed for your old canine companion.

You will need to consider many different factors when you are choosing the bed for your dog. These include:

- Support
- Accessibility
- Temperature
- Size of the Bed and the Dog

Support

A vital element to consider when you are choosing a bed for your senior dog is whether it has enough support for them or not. While soft beds might seem as though they will be more comfortable, if the dog has joint issues and the bed is *too soft*, there is a chance they could sink too deeply. This could cause the dog's joints to rest on the hard floor. This would not be good for them.

Having a bed that's got a bit more firmness to it tends to be a better option, as it will end up providing some additional support. This not only helps the dog's joints, but it also makes it easier for them to get into and out of the bed.

When it comes to support, you will also find there are orthopedic beds available, which are specifically designed to support the joints. Many of these are made from memory foam.

Accessibility

As mentioned, the ability of the dog to get into and out of the bed is important. This is especially true when they are older and not able to move as easily. Not only do you need to think about the support, though. You also have to consider the height of the dog bed. The dog bed should be low enough to the ground that they do not have to step up into or down out of the bed.

You might find some dog beds out there that have rails on them and that are not too dissimilar from human beds with rails. Refrain from getting these, as they can be more trouble than they're worth for the dog trying to get in and out.

If you have a dog that tends to like to have support or "walls" around part of the bed, consider putting the bed in a corner. This way they have actual walls on a couple of sides, but they don't have to step over any rails to get into or out of the bed. It tends to be the best option.

Temperature

One of the other factors that can disrupt sleep is the temperature. Sometimes, the dog can be too cold or too warm. Ensuring that they are a bit warmer tends to be easy. It's possible to add blankets, for example. In addition, some materials will retain heat better, such as many of the memory foam options on the market.

Keep in mind that certain items, such as wool or fleece, will feel nice and soft. However they're going to retain a lot more heat. This might be too much to keep your dog comfortable. Instead, you may want to choose a bed with a fabric cover that is made of cotton, as those fabrics can breathe better and they tend to be a bit cooler. Getting one of the washable waterproof covers mentioned earlier can be a good option to help keep things a bit cooler as well. In addition, it has the added benefit of being waterproof in case the dog has any accidents.

We mentioned that memory foam can retain heat, and that's true. However you can also find gel-infused memory foam that you could use as a cover for the bed. This will add some extra support and this type of foam can help to keep things a bit cooler and more comfortable.

Size of the Bed and the Dog

You will also find that it is important to ensure that the dog's bed is the right size. The biggest problem in this area is choosing a bed that is too small. To ensure that you have a bed of the right size, you can measure your dog from nose to tail, and then add a few extra inches just to be sure.

Of course, you have to think about how your dog likes to sleep, as well. Some dogs, for example, enjoy stretching out a bit when they sleep. Others, however, may prefer sleeping in a rounded or cradled position. This should factor into your decision when you are choosing a size for the dog bed.

In addition, consider the weight of the dog. If you have a dog that is a heavier breed, such as a Mastiff or a Great Dane, you will want to choose a bed that has plenty of cushion, which will ensure that it can support their weight and will not wear out too quickly. This means choosing the right material, as you'll see below.

The Right Material

It is also important for you to consider the type of material that will be used in the bed. There are several different types of materials that are typically used in dog beds and that could be a good option when you are making a choice for your dog. Let's get a closer look at the different types of materials.

Memory Foam

Memory foam has the potential to work well for older dogs, but it needs to be of a high enough quality that it will keep their joints

from touching the floor, even when they are laying down for long periods of time. A thick foam could be a good choice, as it can still be soft while providing a little extra cushion and firmness.

Another benefit of foam is that it tends to keep its shape better, and it won't be "pushed" or "bunched" up on the sides by a dog that moves a lot when they are laying down. Again, this simply provides for some additional protection for the joints. Keep in mind that larger dogs will naturally need to have more foam cushioning, as mentioned above when we discussed the size of the bed.

You will also find that foam tends to hold in heat nicely. This can make it a good choice for older dogs who suffer from arthritis and who might benefit from the extra heat.

Above, we mentioned gel-infused memory foam. These types of covers can provide a nice amount of support and they can help to keep the temperature just right.

What About Heated Beds?

You might have even heard about heated dog beds. There are a range of heated dog beds on the market, and they can work well if you happen to have a dog that gets cold and shivers often. Of course, when you are getting one of these beds, you also have to think about all of the other factors we've discussed when it comes to choosing a dog bed, such as the accessibility and the support, for example.

Consider whether the dog will always need to have a heated bed, as well. During the cooler weather, it might be nice. However, it might not be quite as pleasing for them during the hot weather. While it won't heat up if you don't plug it in, you *still* need to make sure that the material is breathable in that it can stay cool during a hot summer.

Otherwise, you might want to get a heating pad, which you can add to the dog bed when it is cold and take it out the rest of the time.

Waterproof Material

Once again, we'd like to touch on waterproof material. If you have a dog who has accidents, or you believe may have accidents in the future, getting a bed that has waterproof material now is a good option. Many of the dog beds available today already have a waterproof liner. However, that is not the case with all of them

Keep in mind that there are also waterproof covers available in case you already have a good bed in place and just need to waterproof it. If you don't have a way of protecting the material, it can seep into the cushioning and foam. It will then be impossible to get out the scent of urine.

Other Factors to Consider

When you are choosing the dog bed for your canine friends, you will also want to make sure that you choose one that will be easy for you to maintain. Beds tend to get dirty, and you want to make sure that it will not be too time-consuming or difficult for you to keep it clean for your dog. Having a washable cover helps, but you might also want to make sure that the rest of the bed will be easy to clean. Again, waterproof covers can be quite helpful.

When you are choosing a cover for the dog bed, it is important that you find one that is strong and durable. Sure, it needs to be comfortable for the dog. However, it also needs to be one that will not tear easily. Dogs tend to have sharp claws, and as they get older, they move more often in the bed. This could end up putting more stress on the cover. Choose a cover that has some good reviews and that is known as being durable, and you will not have to replace it often.

Watch Your Dog

Once you have chosen a bed that you feel will be a good solution for your senior dog, you still want to watch the dog while they are in the bed. Get a better sense of what they feel about the bed and whether it matches their preferences and their current needs. Keep in mind that the needs of the dog may change as they continue to get older and they have greater and greater needs. You may need to end up changing their bed over time to make sure they are truly comfortable.

Chapter 2: Preventing and Dealing With Common Medical Conditions of Older Dogs – The Basics

Earlier in the book, we touched briefly on some of the various medical conditions and issues that older dogs face.

In this chapter, we will cover some of the basic elements that you will want to consider when it comes to treating your dog for various conditions. Later in the book, we will look more deeply into different conditions that could be affecting your dog and what you can do about them.

Alternative Medicines

When your senior dog is ill, and your current veterinarian is not able to provide you with any workable solutions that help your canine friend, you might want to consider checking out some of the alternative medicine options available.

Some of these therapies, some of which are discussed in the following chapter, include:

- *Acupuncture* – One of the treatments that has started to garner more attention is acupuncture. This is an ancient practice from Chinese medicine that has been used in humans, as well as animals. It utilizes needles being placed into the skin by professionals at "meridians", which are supposed to create a change in the body. Those who utilize this type of therapy believe that it can help older dogs who are dealing with weakness, dysfunction of the organs, cancer, cognitive problems, incontinence, arthritis, and more.

- *Massage* – Another type of therapy utilized by certain veterinary professionals for canines is massage. Canine massage can help to provide relaxation for an animal, just as it can a human. It is believed that it can also provide help when it comes to dealing with pain, promote healing, and can even help with relaxation and provide mental benefits similar to those achieved with acupuncture.

- *Herbal Medicine* – Another area that some owners are considering is herbal medicine. Again, this has been popular in the human community as well. However, you have to be very careful about what you give your dog. If you're going to use herbal medicine, it should only be those items that you have researched, spoken to your vet about, and that have been deemed safe for your canine companion.

- *Hydrotherapy* – This type of therapy is being used more and more with dogs who are suffering from orthopedic conditions, arthritis, and muscle injuries. There are some proponents of this type of therapy that believe it can also be helpful for dogs suffering from mental problems. They believe it has calming effects on these dogs.

These are some of the most popular types of alternative therapies that are in existence currently, but they are not the only ones. Chances are, more and more will crop up over time. One of the important things to remember when it comes to these alternative therapies is that not all dogs are going to respond favorably. In some cases, the dog won't have any improvement at all. Other times, however, these types of therapies and remedies have proven to be useful.

As we stated previously, before you provide any type of treatment or change to their routine, therapies, or diet, it is very important that you speak with a professional veterinarian. Failure to do so could put your dog in danger, which is the last thing you want.

Choosing the Right Diet

Dogs will have different nutritional needs, and this is certainly true when it comes to senior dogs. When your dog becomes a canine senior citizen, it can often be difficult to understand the changes in their dietary requirements. Even though they might've spent most of their life eating certain types of food, including food that they might still enjoy, age can catch up with them.

This means you need to pay attention to what they are eating and work to create a quality, healthy diet for them. If you don't, there is always the chance that what they are eating could cause them problems with their digestive health, as well as affect other areas of their health.

So, what should you offer your senior dog?

One of the things that you will want to keep in mind is that even though some of the bags of dog food out there might say that they are for senior dogs or for "all stages of life", that does not always mean they have different ingredients. Sometimes, it is just the packaging that is different. This is because there are no regulations with dog food that requires that their claims for senior dogs are accurate.

When you are creating the diet for your dog, you will want to consider some of the main factors that should be considered.

Nutritional Needs

The nutritional needs for senior dogs do tend to be somewhat different from younger dogs. While all dogs need to have quite a bit of protein in the diet, senior dogs will often need more. Having extra protein will provide the additional amino acids needed by the dog, and having extra protein could also help with healing.

Experts believe that senior dog diets should end up having about 75g of protein for every 1000 calories provided to the dog. However, if the dog has kidney disease, this is not always possible. One of the reasons for this is that the phosphorus content tends to increase, which is undesirable. Therefore, you want to find ways to restrict the phosphorus.

The amount of fat that should be in the dog's diet can vary, as well. If the dog tends to be getting thinner as they get older, then it might be advisable to increase the fat content in the diet. Of course, the opposite also holds true. If the dog has a problem with obesity, you will likely want to reduce the fat content and the overall calories in the diet.

Make Sure It Is Digestible

As a dog gets older, they tend to become more susceptible to conditions related to their digestion. This means that an older dog might suffer from colitis, inflammatory bowel disease, or they might develop a food allergy.

To determine if your dog has any problems with their diet, the best thing to do is watch for any changes in their behavior after they've eaten. Do they not like certain types of food now? Do they have digestive issues after they've eaten a certain type of food? You will want to change the diet and consider using fresh foods, which tend to be easier for the body to break down.

Dental Needs

If you have a senior dog, you might've noticed some issues with their teeth, even if you have taken proper care of those teeth and brushed them throughout the years.

Older dogs can sometimes lose teeth even when they been taken care of properly. It happens. Therefore, you have to think about the food that they are eating to make sure it is a good solution for their dental situation.

For example, kibble, even though the dog might've been eating that their entire life, can be difficult for senior dogs. If those dogs have sore teeth, loose teeth, or infected teeth, they will not be able to chew properly. The pieces can be hard to break up.

Sometimes, this leads to the dog "wolfing" down their food. Essentially, they swallow it without chewing. This can be unhealthy for them. In other circumstances, the dog will instead refuse to eat. This will cause them to lose weight and they could eventually have other health problems.

One of the ways to combat this problem is by moistening the food with water, or gravy, for example. This makes it softer and easier to eat. Another option would be to start feeding only soft food.

Does the Food Have Added Supplements?

When you are looking through the various dog food options that are on the market, you will notice that some of them may make claims that they have supplements added to them. For example, there are some types of dog food that claim to have glucosamine and similar supplements in them. Unfortunately, many of the dog foods that claim to have supplements in them will not have enough of those substances to be very effective.

Therefore, if the dog is having certain issues, such as joint problems, you would want to choose a dog food that is specifically labeled for that health condition. Another option would be to add to these supplements to the food on your own.

You could also add supplements such as DHA, and omega-3 fatty acid, antioxidants, and medium-chain triglycerides. If you're going to add the supplements the food, make sure you understand the proper amount to add for a dog sized like yours. Talking with a veterinarian to get advice on this will be your best option.

Hydration

Of course, proper hydration is also essential for your dog's diet, as we've mentioned earlier in the book. Make sure that your dog has access to clean, fresh water, and if they are not drinking properly, you can moisten their food to help provide them with some additional hydration.

Talk with the Vet About Dietary Needs

As always, a veterinarian will be the best source of knowledge when it comes to determining the exact nutritional needs for your senior dog. Talk with your veterinarian and see what they recommend. There is no "one true answer" that will work for all dogs out there. Each dog is an individual, and that means you and the vet will need to judge their nutritional needs individually to come up with the proper diet.

In addition, the veterinarian will be able to let you know whether the specialized foods you are considering for your dog are worth your money are not.

How Do the Vets Know?

Typically, a veterinarian will look at the symptoms that your dog has shown to help determine what needs to be done with their diet. For example, if the dog is constipated, the vet might suggest that you offer food that has extra fiber. If the dog is suffering from behavioral changes, they might recommend using supplements

in the food, such as medium-chain triglycerides, fish oil, and antioxidants. If the dog suffers from chronic pancreatitis, they may recommend that the fat content in the diet is lowered.

Creating a Friendly Living Environment

In addition to providing the right types of treatment and a good diet, one of the most essential and basic elements of keeping your senior dog happy and healthy is providing a friendly living environment.

Of course, you might be wondering just what this means in terms of your dog. Here are a few simple tips that you will want to follow.

Keep the Dog Nearby

Remember, dogs are pack animals. This means they want to be with their pack, which is *you and your family* in this case. Therefore, you don't want to keep the senior dog hidden away. Keep them close.

Even though you might want to have the dog's bed in a comfortable and warm location, you don't want a dog that rests most of the day to feel like they have to be in another room away from everyone. This is not good for their mental health, and they could even feel as if they have done something wrong.

The best option is to have a secondary bed located in the area where the family tends to spend a lot of time. This way, he or she can be with you, even though they might just be lounging around and sleeping most of the time. They will feel better knowing that they are still a part of the family.

Keep the Dog Comfortable

Along the same lines, you will always want to make sure that your senior dog is as comfortable as possible. This means providing them with comfortable places to rest and quiet places where they can spend time if they wish. You will want to attempt to keep the home environment as consistent as possible, as well, or it can upset them. This is especially true if the dog is suffering from cognitive issues.

You will want to retrain from rearranging the furniture in the home, for example. You will also want to keep the sleeping areas and feeding locations the same, as well. By keeping things the same, it will reduce the risk of confusion that the dog might otherwise suffer.

Make It Easy for Them

Earlier, we discussed some of the things that you can do when you are trying to help make the life of the dog easier, such as keeping the dog bed in an area that's close to their food and water, and the door to take them outside, and to put runners or carpets on the floor and stairs to make it easier for them to walk without fear of slipping.

Consider what you might do to make your home easier to live in for a senior human, and then adapt those ideas for your dog. There are many parallels.

Make Sure Kids and Other Animals Behave

As your dog gets older, they might not be in the mood to play as much as they did when they were younger. They don't have the energy, and they might be in pain in some cases. This means that they don't want to have kids hanging all over them and tugging at them, and they don't want to have younger dogs or other pets trying to "ruffle their feathers", so to speak. You will want to let any children in the family know that they need to be extra gentle with their old friend, and you will want to keep an eye on other pets and how they are interacting with the dog.

If those other pets are not being gentle and if they are truly bothering the dog, you will want to do your best to keep them separated. If you don't, it will end up putting undue stress on the senior dog. In addition, the older dog might end up snapping at the other animals, or people, if they are continually bothered or injured.

Chapter 3: The Joints of Older Dogs

Dogs that are getting on in their years will often have problems with their joints, just like people tend to do. Dogs spend quite a bit of their lives running and jumping and having a good old time. They can put a lot of wear and tear on their joints, and over time, this can lead to problems. More use means that there is a greater chance of injuries and problems later in life.

Problems with the Joints

Some of the more common types of joint issues that occur with dogs include developing osteoarthritis and suffering from ACL tears. If the dog also has hip or elbow dysplasia, the joint will not necessarily develop correctly in the first place. However, the main problem in older dogs tends to come from degeneration through use. Many older dogs suffer from arthritis and they are in a substantial amount of pain.

There are two different types of potential joint problems, though. Not only may the dog be suffering from pain because of arthritis, but they could also be in pain because of trauma or developmental disorders.

Based on research from the American Veterinary Medical Association, veterinarians claim that an estimated 90% of dogs who are older, typically eight years and up, will suffer from at least some form of joint paint. In fact, even dogs that are considered to be in their middle-age can suffer. According to the same research, around 20% of these middle-aged dogs will have joint problems.

Yet, dogs don't have the capacity to tell people just how much pain they are suffering. Therefore, you need to do a good job of understanding that pain, recognizing the signs, and finding ways that you can make it better for your furry friend.

Joint issues can affect many areas in a dog's body. The most common ones include:

- Knees
- Elbows
- Hips
- Lower back
- Paw wrists

Dealing With Pain

If you have an elderly dog that is not moving quite as spryly as they did when they were younger, it is natural. They are older and they've slowed down. However, they might also be suffering from serious joint issues, as mentioned. You will want to have an understanding of how you can understand whether your dog is in pain and what you can do to help them.

Signs of Pain

One of the reasons that it is often difficult to recognize the signs of joint pain in dogs is because many of them will instinctively hide pain. This is an inherited trait, as they do not want to appear weak to predators or even members of their pack. In this case, you are a member of the pack.

However, as the pain grows more pronounced and as a dog gets older, it will typically become easier to recognize the signs and symptoms of pain. Some of the most prevalent include:

- *Lameness* – When a dog is suffering from lameness, you may notice that they have an odd normal stance or that they move differently than they once did. Just because the dog might be suffering from what seems to be lameness, it is not a certainty that they are suffering from a joint problem, but it could be an indicator that joint issues are beginning.

- *Inactivity* – You might also notice that the dog is no longer as active as they once were. While this is normal as a dog gets older, having reluctance or a refusal to move, get up, or exercise could be an indicator that there is joint pain.

- *Stiffness* – The dog might also move in a stiff manner, and it can take them longer to get "up and running" so to speak.

- *Restless Pacing* – While many dogs will want to move less and less as their joints are in more pain, that is not always the case. You might find that you have a dog that gets up and paces back and forth restlessly, as if they are unable to find a position where they are comfortable.

- *Shivering* – In some cases, you might notice that the dog shivers, typically when they are standing and trying to walk or move. This is not always because they are cold. It could be due to the pain that they are feeling.

- *Refusal to Play* – When the joints are in pain, it also typically means that the dog will not want to move and play like they did when they were younger. This is true even when you might be trying to get them to play their favorite game.

- *Refusal to Eat* – In some cases, the pain could be so bad that the dog actually does not want to eat any longer. The refusal to eat could end up being severe enough that it causes the dog to lose weight, which leads to muscle atrophy, noted below.

- *Sensitivity When Being Pet in Certain Areas* – As you pet your dog, watch for indications that there is increased sensitivity when you are petting them. When dogs suffering from joint pain are touched near the sore joints, they will likely react. In some cases, they will pull away in pain. However, you might also notice that they growl or that they even snap at you. They aren't doing this because they don't like you. They are doing this because the pain causes an instinctual reaction to snap like that.

- *Reduced Range of Motion* – As the dog moves, you will also likely notice that they don't have the same range of motion that they once did. This goes beyond just the stiffness mentioned earlier. It means that the animal is physically unable to move their joints past a certain point.

- *Crepitus in the Joints* – The term *crepitus* simply means a noise or a vibration that occurs in the body when scar tissue is rubbing against other scar tissue. It can create a popping sound and a grating sound. If this happens often when the dog gets up and moves, it could be an indicator of issues with the joints.

- *Muscle Atrophy* – The muscles of the dog could become atrophied due to nonuse along with not getting enough food to help maintain them properly. Atrophied muscles make the dog weaker.

- *Altered Behavior* – You might also notice that your dog's general behavior is changing, and this can be due to painful joints, as well. You know your dog better than anyone else does, and if you notice that there are shifts in their behavior, joint pain could be one of the causes. However, joint problems are not necessarily the only cause of changed behavior in your dog, as you will learn later in the book.

It is important to remember that even though the above signs and symptoms are often indicators of joint pain, the symptoms above could also be indicators of other health problems that the dog could be dealing with. The vet will be able to help rule out other diseases to make sure the dog gets the proper care. By noting these signs and symptoms, it can help to ensure that your dog gets the proper care when needed.

Keep in mind that there are things that can be done to help with joint pain, even though there is no cure for osteoarthritis. This means you will want to make sure that you consider your options with your vet.

Below are some of the common methods that can be used to help your dog with this type of pain. Finding a treatment plan that works well for your dog can help to improve their quality of life substantially.

Common Pain Medications

In the past, there were only a few medications that were able to treat pain in dogs reliably and effectively. However, today, there are far more options available.

When it comes to the treatment of joint pain and arthritis in dogs, NSAIDs tend to be the go-to method. These are nonsteroidal anti-inflammatory drugs, and they help to reduce the pain from arthritis, along with stiffness and inflammation. Overall, these medications tend to improve the quality of life for dogs who are suffering from this condition with their joints.

In the past, treating joint pain in dogs was typically left to low-dose aspirin. The nonsteroidal anti-inflammatory drugs tend to work much better for pain, but they do have some potential side effects.

The goal of the NSAIDs is to inhibit the effects of the prostaglandins, which can cause inflammation. However, they also suppress the other functions of that enzyme, which includes helping with the blood circulation to the kidneys and the production of blood platelets, to name a few things.

This can cause NSAID toxicity, and it can cause a range of side effects.

Some of those side effects include:

- Digestive tract issues, such as irritation to the stomach lining, ulcers, and perforations in the stomach and intestines.
- Because of the change to the prostaglandins, there could be issues with the kidneys as well. Namely, it could cause a reduced blood flow.
- Liver damage can occur as well. The types of side effects that occur in the liver can be divided into two categories. The first is dose-dependent toxicity, which means the higher the dose the worse the damage to the liver. This will typically only occur if there is a large overdose of the NSAID. The second category is dose-independent liver toxicity. This means the issue can occur regardless of how low the dose might be. This could occur when a dog has an abnormal sensitivity to the medication.

If you notice that your dog has any of the following signs after they are taking NSAIDs, you will want to discontinue their use and get in touch with your vet to see if the medication could be the cause of the problem.

- Decrease or increase in appetite
- Decrease or increase in thirst
- Aggression
- Seizure
- Confusion
- Lethargy
- Vomiting

- Diarrhea or black, tarry, or bloody stools
- Yellowing of the skin, gums, or eyes
- Red, itchy skin
- Change in the dog's urinary habits – this includes changes in the frequency of urination, as well as the color or the smell of the urine

It is important that the veterinarian recommends the NSAIDs and that you do not self-diagnose your dog. In addition, you don't want to just put ibuprofen from your medicine cabinet in with the dog's food. Human medications and dosages can be toxic for dogs. It tends to be a better option to make sure that you are using a quality medication that is recommended for canines.

Some of the common options for dogs include:

- *Rimadyl* – This is a very common and widely prescribed NSAID. Typically, it is given once per day. It is available through caplets, chewable tablets, as well as injection.
- *Deramaxx* – This can be used in dogs that are over four pounds, and it is typically used to help with postoperative pain. However, it can also be used to help with inflammation of the joints.
- *Metacam* – This medication is available as an oral suspension or as an injectable.
- *Zubrin* – This table disintegrates in the mouth of the dog. There are indications that this medication may also have a lower risk of side effects of intestinal ulceration.
- *Previcox* – This is a chewable tablet that has been used with success in dogs who are suffering from arthritis. It has been shown to work quickly and effectively in these dogs.
- *Novox* – This medication is currently available in caplet form, and it is a generic version of carprofen.

These are some of the common medications that are provided to help with the pain that dogs are feeling due to their joint problems. Whenever your vet decides to prescribe any meds for your dogs, make sure that you ask them more about the drugs in question and get a better idea of exactly what the medication is supposed to do and what side effects he could have for your dog. After all, you want to know what you should be looking for in case there is a problem.

Supplements

In addition to the use of pain medications that are prescribed by the vet, many owners are turning to various types of supplements that can be used to help improve the condition of their dog's joints. As always, you will want to make sure you consult with your vet before providing any supplements for the dog just to be on the safe side.

Some of the common supplements that are used to help with joint problems for your dog include:

- *Fish Oil and Omega-3* – The Journal of the American Veterinary Medical Association published a study that showed dogs who are suffering from osteoarthritis and who were given omega-3 had a significant improvement in as little as six weeks when compared with dogs that were given a placebo. After 12 weeks, the dogs that were taking the omega-3 supplements had improvements that were even more noticeable.

- *Glucosamine and Chondroitin* – Humans have been using these supplements to improve their joints for many years now. This supplement is starting to become far more common in the treatment of arthritis in pets, including both dogs and cats. These supplements can help to stimulate cartilage production. They have also been shown to help provide benefits for dogs who have hip dysplasia. You will find that these ingredients are found in many of the dog joint supplements on the market today.

As you can see, these have the potential to provide your dog with more relief from their pain. With a large number of supplements on the market today the claim to provide joint relief for your dogs, and that include these ingredients, you need to do your research. You want to learn which ones are the highest recommended from other owners like yourself.

Of course, you can also get some insight from your veterinarian. Just be somewhat cautious if they are selling the supplements directly through their office, as it means they're making money directly through those sales. Make sure that the supplements they are recommending truly are high-quality before you give them to your dog.

Acupuncture

Earlier, we touched on acupuncture as one of the alternative therapies that is often used with dogs today. If your canine companion is suffering from joint problems, this might be an avenue you want to pursue, as well.

When you are choosing a person to provide the acupuncture for your dog, it is important that you first take the time to research the acupuncture specialists in your area and make sure that you are working with someone who specializes in dogs. After all, dogs and people are very different not only in their physiology, but also how they will react to this type of treatment.

People are able to understand and rationalize that they need to have treatments to help improve their health. Dogs are unable to do this. This means that your dog may not take kindly to a stranger poking and prodding them with needles. It could cause them to become more stressed out or it can even cause them to bite the person trying to perform the acupuncture.

You know your dog and how they react with strangers and the vet. This can help to give you a better idea of whether your dog will respond favorably to the act of getting the needles placed into them. If you know that your dog will not react well, then you may want to choose another form of treatment.

Make sure that the canine acupuncturists not only have experience working with dogs, but also that they have a *good reputation* in the field. This is an alternative form of medicine, and that means that there are often charlatans trying to work in the area who might not really know what they're doing. Always take time to make sure you're working with the very best. Your dog deserves it.

Massage

Massage has similarities to acupuncture when it comes to understanding exactly how your dog is going to deal with the effects of the actual treatment itself, namely, having a massage on joints that could be sore. Still, professionals who can offer proper canine massage and who may be able to teach you how to give your dog a massage to help relieve the joints, can be a huge benefit.

It can help to bond more with your dog, and it can provide you with some relatively simple techniques that can help your dog to find some relief from pain, even if just for a little while.

You can also learn how to provide basic canine massage on your own and through online manuals and videos. Once you learn the proper technique, it is a good idea to provide your dog with a massage at a minimum of three times per week for at least 10 to 15 minutes each massage. If possible, increase this frequency to daily. If you spend time with your dog regularly and are petting them, it should be relatively easy to find the time to massage them.

Again, if your dog is particularly sensitive and has joints that are in extreme pain, the massage could cause them to snap and bite without them thoroughly realizing what they're doing. In that case, utilizing more than just one of these methods for dealing with joint pain is important.

For example, you could ensure that they are taking pain medication to help deal with their joint pain and then slowly supplement with massage. This way, they are not in as much pain to start, which means they are less likely to feel extreme pain and bite. Also, you should start with shorter sessions and then work your way upward. Even just a minute or two in the beginning can help. Then, you can work up to five minutes, 10 minutes, and then 15 minutes.

When providing massage for the dog, whether it is you or a professional who is giving massage, it is important that it is always done in a calm and peaceful setting. In addition, you never want to overwork one body part. Overworking a part of the body with massage could actually lead to further inflammation in that area. That is the last thing you want.

For dogs that have problematic joints, the evening and the early morning tend to be the best times to provide the massage. In addition if they have had a day that has been particularly active, then you might want to give a massage as soon as they have a chance to rest.

You should be capable of providing your dog with a basic massage. However, if you believe the dog needs a deep tissue massage or that they need additional pain relief through massage, it should only be provided by a canine massage professional.

Prosthetics

In some cases, the condition of the dog's joints can deteriorate to a point where it becomes extremely difficult for them to walk and move around as easily as they once did. In those cases, it might appear that they essentially lose the use of one or more of their limbs.

If that's the case, you might want to consider canine wheelchairs and similar prosthetics, such as braces and splints for their legs. These can help to ensure that your dog can still have some form of activity, even though it might not be the same as it was before.

Exercise

One of the reasons that some dogs have more joint problems than others, and the reason that some younger dogs can suffer from joint problems, is because they are not getting enough exercise. This can cause their weight to increase to dangerous levels, which puts undue stress on those joints.

If you have a dog that is overweight, whether they are old and not, it is a good idea to increase the amount of exercise they get regularly. This, along with diet, which is discussed next, will help to reduce the stress that is placed upon the joints. With less stress, it means they tend to be in less pain.

Humans can suffer from similar problems. Those who are heavier will have more problems with their joints as they get older. This is because there is additional wear and tear on the joints and cartilage because of the weight.

While this might not be the thing that is causing the problem with the joints, this is something that you as a dog owner can take care of. Provide your dog with enough exercise to remain healthy and within their ideal weight range.

However, if they are already suffering from joint problems, you will want to make sure that you are providing them with exercise that is not going to put any undue stress on those joints. Some walks, along with swimming, can work well for your dog. Take it easier and combine their exercise plan with diet, as noted below, to help relieve the pressure on their joints.

Diet

Along the same lines as exercise, you will want to be careful about what your dog is eating to make sure that they do not put on too much weight, which could cause problems with their joints.

However, you will also want to think about the kinds of food that you are providing for your beloved pet, as some could actually help or harm their joints.

What the Dog Needs

Ideally, you will want to make sure that your dog has a diet that is high in quality protein, and most of that protein should come from beef, poultry, and fish. Eggs and cheese could be added, as well. The increased amount of amino acids that the dog is getting through additional protein may be able to help with the symptoms associated with arthritis.

Having too many carbs could actually end up leading to weight gain. This is because the amount of nutrition provided through a high carbohydrate diet is not equal to the number of calories that the dog is getting. They eat more calories that are essentially useless, and they gain unhealthy weight.

In addition, you will want to make sure that you avoid grains and starches. These not only have increased calories, but they can also cause fluctuations in the dog's blood sugar levels and they have the potential to cause swelling. Certain types of vegetables, such as potatoes and eggplant, could even increase the arthritis symptoms that dogs suffer.

Try to make sure that the foods you are providing for the dog include calcium, magnesium, and vitamin D. *All three* of these need to be provided. The vitamin D will help the dog's body to absorb the calcium, which will help to grow and strengthen bones. You'll find that many different types of dairy products, as well as fish and beef, can provide vitamin D.

The magnesium will help with many of the various body processes. This includes regulation of blood sugar levels, as well as helping the nerves and muscles function properly. It also helps the dog's body to absorb calcium. One of the best sources of magnesium is meat. This is why having a high-protein meat-based diet is so important for the dog

Foods to Avoid

Simply by removing grains from the dog's diet, you will find it can often help to improve their arthritis conditions, since grains are known to cause inflammation. However, there are some other types of food that you will want to be careful of when it comes to your dog's diet, as well.

- *Make sure salt intake is moderate* – This means don't add any sugar, spices, or salt to anything the dog eats that is already high in salt or sugar.
- *Avoid plant-based oils* – Plant-based oils include sunflower oil, corn oil, and vegetable oil. These contain arachidonic acid. This is an omega-6 fatty acid. Unlike the healthy omega-3 fatty acids, this can lead to increased inflammation in the body.
- *Avoid fatty meat* – Even though we mentioned that your dog should have a diet that is high in meat, you don't want to give the dog meat that is too fatty. Always try to find leaner cuts of meat for the dog. Fish can also be a good choice, as it is lean and it has omega-3 fatty acids.
- *Avoid citrus fruit* – While it is safe for the dog to eat this type of fruit, citrus tends to aggravate the symptoms of arthritis.

While there are a number of foods on the market that claim to be a good option for dogs who are suffering from arthritis and joint problems, this doesn't mean that they are all a good option for your dog. Always make sure you check the ingredients first. If you notice that the top ingredient – or one of the top ingredients – is grain or wheat, you want to avoid it. In some cases, people may want to make their own dog food. While it will take longer, you can be certain of what your dog is eating.

Therapies to Avoid

The therapies mentioned in this chapter have a chance at helping your dog to deal with their joint problems. However, this does not mean that all therapies are going to be worth your time.

Before you consider any type of therapy for your dog, whether it is for their joints or any other issue they could be facing, do your research. Make sure that there is a good foundation for this type of therapy and that others have been able to achieve measurable results for the dog. Don't waste your time, and don't do anything that could be dangerous for the dog.

For example, there is a land of promise when it comes to stem cell therapy for dogs who have osteoarthritis. However, the studies are very limited, and it is unclear exactly how effective it will be. This type of treatment would be very costly, of course. It might be more sensible to wait until it is a *proven* therapy.

Quality-of-Life Considerations

You dog has certain needs that need to be respected, provided for, and recognized. The quality of life of the dog is one of the things that you need to watch when it comes to illness in your dog. This is true whether that illness comes through joint problems or other health conditions.

A veterinary oncologist named Dr. Alice Villalobos created a quality-of-life scale for dogs that can be used to help get a better idea of just how the dog is coping in their current condition. This scale can be used not only for joint problems, but for other issues, as well, as you will see.

This scale considers several different factors in your dog's life, as noted below. Each of these are to be determined on a scale of one to 10. You want the final tally to be as low as possible.

Hurt

You do not want your pet to be in a lot of pain. Proper pain control, including the ability to breathe properly, is essential. There are methods of controlling pain, as noted earlier in this chapter, and you want to keep the pain in your dog low and bearable. Based on how your dog is acting, and how you have been able to do to reduce that pain, you will then give it a rating of one to 10.

Hunger

If the dog is unable to continue eating properly, you can try to hand feed them. If this is not possible, you may want to consider a feeding tube. Another option would be to try blended or liquid diets. Based on how well the dog can eat, you will again provide a rating on the scale.

Hydration

Along the same lines, you want to consider the hydration of the dog. We've discussed some ways to help improve the dog's hydration earlier.

Hygiene

As some dogs get older, their hygiene deteriorates. This is true even when their owners attempt to help improve their hygiene. There are some ways and methods of providing hygiene even to pets that might be bedridden. There are methods that can be used to keep them clean and dry. However, it is also important to consider exactly how diminished the dog's quality-of-life is at this stage.

Happiness

Does the dog still have any joy or mental stimulation? Keep in mind that dogs communicate through their tails, as well as with their eyes. Does the dog still interact with members of the family and with the environment? You can, as mentioned earlier, place the bed near where the rest of the family spends most of their time, and this can help. However, there may come a time when the dog simply does not respond to exterior stimulus, and they seem very withdrawn.

Mobility

The mobility of the dog should be measured, as well. Osteoarthritis and injury can affect the movement of the dog, of course. Using the tips from this chapter and mobility devices can help to increase the mobility of the dog, allowing them to stay more active. Veterinarians tend to be very important when it comes to taking care of the mobility issues of your dog.

More Good Days than Bad

With all dogs having health problems, there tend to be both good days and bad days. It is very important for the owner to keep an eye on the dog and see how many good days in a row they have and how many bad days.

Bad days can mean different things depending on the condition and disease, of course. For example, bad days might include those days when the dog seems to be in a substantial amount of pain, when they have trouble breathing, when they are nauseous and vomiting, and when they simply can't move.

As much as you love your dog, and as much as they are a part of your family, when it gets to the point where their quality-of-life is suffering, you need to think about their needs over yours. This means that you may need to make some very difficult decisions regarding your dog.

What to Do With Your Dog When the Quality of Their Life Does Start to Suffer

If you find that your dog's quality-of-life is very low, it might be time to consider euthanasia, as difficult as this may be. We will discuss more about dealing with the end-of-life for your pet later in the book.

To help you get a better understanding of the current quality-of-life of your dog, and what you may need to do, you will want to speak with – you guessed it – your dog's veterinarian.

They can provide you with the best insight as to what you can do to make your dog's life as good and peaceful as it can possibly be based on the current condition of the pet. In addition, they can discuss with you the options you have available at the end of the animal's life.

Later in the book, we'll be discussing more about the end of life for the dog and how you can make the right decision for your beloved canine companion. It is never an easy time, but hopefully, we can at least shine a light on a subject that you will need to think about.

Chapter 4: Psychological Changes in the Dog

While the physical changes that occur in your dog tend to be easy to see – the greying of the fur, the slowness in the way they move, for example – there are also potential mental changes that can occur with your dog, as well. These types of issues can be just as severe, and you will want to watch your dog as closely for these types of changes as you would any changes to their physical well-being.

It can be very difficult to see your faithful companion suffer various mental health issues, as they get older.

Anxiety and Fear

Although it is certainly possible for anxiety and fear to be a problem with dogs of any age, it can become more problematic and pronounced as a dog gets older and less sure of things in their surroundings. In fact, one of the first signs of mental problems and dementia with a dog is anxiety. They can become confused and frightened without any real indicator as to what triggered the problem.

The fear and the anxiety that the dog feels could be caused through a diminished mental state. However, there are other issues that could be at play with the elderly dogs, as well.

For example, as the dog gets older, their hearing and vision is not as good as it once was. This causes the dog to be more easily startled. In addition, the physical pain that the dog might be going through, such as having painful joints, can cause them to be more fearful and anxious. They may believe that more things are going to cause them pain and will make them wary. In addition, the anxiousness and fear that a dog is experiencing can also be due to medications.

The anxiety and fear can manifest in different ways and behavioral changes. Some of the most common and relatively subtle ways include:

- Hiding
- Solitude
- Seeking Comfort
- Shaking
- Panting
- Excessive Chewing or Licking

However, there are often other symptoms of anxiety and fear, as well. Some of the most common of these include:

- Excessive Barking
- Aggression
- Trying to escape
- Hyperactivity
- Defecation or Urination Indoors (although this could be a sign or a symptom of other health problems, as well)
- Destruction of Items in the Home
- Panic Attacks

The Mind of the Ill and the Elderly Dog

When the dog gets older and when they are ill, their brain doesn't respond the same way it did when they were younger. As mentioned, they may be more anxious and more fearful. It may get to the point where you feel as though you barely recognize your dog on some days. In fact, they can get to the point where they barely seem to recognize *you*.

This is very difficult for the dog and for you. When a dog starts to suffer from these types of problems, it can cause a range of behavioral changes in them.

Dementia

Dementia can affect dogs, just as it does humans. Clinically, this is known as canine cognitive dysfunction or CCD. The deterioration of brain tissue in the dog causes changes in their personality, changes in their normal activity, and it can cause memory loss. There are many similarities between the conditions and symptoms a dog faces and those that a human who is suffering from dementia goes through.

The Symptoms of Canine Dementia

It can often be difficult to identify the symptoms of canine dementia because there are a number of potential symptoms, and they can be misread as symptoms of other health issues for the dog.

Still, if you have an older dog, it is a good idea to have an understanding of some of the symptoms. If you notice these, you can talk with your vet about them.

- Aggression
- Anorexia, where the dog will not eat or drink
- Abnormal behavior
- Circling

- Increased barking or whining
- Disorientation
- Disrupted sleep cycle
- Excitement
- Fixed stare – this fixed stare is usually at a wall or a door, not anything that would typically excite a dog.
- Getting stuck in various places
- Incontinence
- Lack of interest
- Skin sensitivity

What Are the Causes?

Currently, there aren't any known causes for canine dementia. The only factor that seems to be consistent is that it happens with dogs as they are older and entering their senior years. It does not seem to be specific toward any breed or gender. Dogs that are 11 or older may start to show signs of dementia. You will find that the majority of dogs that are 16 years old or older show signs of dementia.

It is very important that you take note of the changes in behavior that your dog is going through and that you let the veterinarian know about these changes. If you do not have this information, the veterinarian will not likely do any testing or evaluation because they won't have any clinical reason to assume that the dog has dementia.

Once they provide you with a diagnosis, they can start to provide treatments that can help.

What Are Treatments?

It is important to note that there are no cures for dementia. However, there are certain things that can be done to provide a more comfortable environment for the dog and to make them feel better and safer.

Diet

There is evidence that certain changes to the diet, such as the addition of antioxidants, can help to slow the process of brain degeneration. Remember, a proper and high-quality diet is important at every stage of the dog's life.

The Environment

Environmental changes are important to consider, as well. While at home, you will keep things the same whenever possible. This means that you want to avoid making any big changes, such as rearranging the furniture or moving to a new place if you can help it. These large types of changes can be very jarring to dogs, and that is *especially* true if those dogs are suffering from dementia.

Earlier, we mentioned that sometimes the dog might get stuck in various places and have trouble maneuvering. Because they are not able to navigate obstacles as easily as they once were, it is very important to attempt to keep their main living space clean and free of clutter. Beware of any areas that could cause problems for them.

It tends to be a good idea to try to follow a predictable daily routine with your dog who is suffering from dementia. If there do need to be changes to that routine, make them slowly rather than sudden.

If you have other dogs, make sure that you are ready to keep your dog suffering from dementia away from the other dogs. There is the risk that they might not respond properly in dog social situations, which could end up leading to a fight between the dogs and unnecessary injuries.

Brain Stimulation

You will want to make an effort to attempt to stimulate the brain of your dog as you notice the cognitive decline. By stimulating the brain with frequent walks, by trying to teach them new tricks, and playing with the dog, it can help to keep their interest and help to slow the crawl of dementia.

Medications

The veterinarian might decide to prescribe the dog some medication. For example, they may look for medications that can help to increase and build up the amount of dopamine that the dog has in their brain. This is because dementia tends to be marked by a lower amount of dopamine. Some veterinarians might also recommend supplementation through ginkgo biloba, which is something that humans utilize as a means to regulate dopamine and to increase blood flow to the brain.

Depending on where you live, the veterinarian might also recommend the use of CBD oil. This is an alternative medication that can help with anxiety and other issues that dementia can cause. There are even certain pet stores that carry this. Melatonin is an option that can work, as well, as it can help to relax the dog.

A Difficult Time

Having a dog that is dealing with dementia will be difficult whether or not you have other pets or young family members that don't entirely understand what is happening. It can sometimes be difficult to predict exactly what's going to happen with your dog from one day to the next, and you don't know whether they're going to have a good day or a bad day.

Because this can be such a hard time, you will want to make sure you have a good working relationship with your vet, and that you can trust them to try different methods of helping with the dementia issue. You also want to be sure that they will be honest with you when it comes to the quality of life of your dog.

Chapter 5: Canine Seizures

Seizures are another serious issue that can affect your dog. These seizures can occur in dogs of varying ages, and certainly not only in older dogs. If a dog is suffering from epilepsy, it means that they have uncontrolled and abnormal bursts of electrical activity in their brain. This is what causes seizures. They can affect how the dog behaves. If the dog suffers from these often, they could be suffering from a seizure disorder.

The seizures might look like a twitch in the dog's body or face, or it could appear to be uncontrollable shaking. This shaking or twitching can last a few seconds, a minute, or it could last up to several minutes. This can be frightening for both you and your dog, especially if you have never seen it happen before.

What Can Cause Seizures in Canines?

There is no single cause that might be responsible for seizures. However, one of the most common types of seizures in dogs is known as idiopathic epilepsy. This is an inherited condition, but the true cause of it is still unknown. There are plenty of other causes of seizures, as well.

Some of the most common include:
- Kidney Disease
- Ingestion of Poison
- Liver Disease
- Blood Sugar that is Too Low or Too High
- Issues with the Electrolytes in the Body
- Anemia
- Head Injury
- Encephalitis
- Stroke
- Brain Cancer

As you can see, some of these conditions that could lead to seizures tend to be more common in older dogs. For example, kidney disease, anemia, and head injuries are typically seen more often in older dogs. Older dogs might also have infections in the brain or metabolic causes that would increase the risk of seizures.

Common Symptoms of Seizures

As with humans, the exact symptoms can vary from one dog to another. The most common tends to be shaking, as mentioned. The dog may have stiffened muscles, they could collapse, they may drool, they may chomp or chew on their tongue, they could foam at the mouth, and they may even lose consciousness.

In some cases, when they fall over their legs will continue to move similar to how they might "run" when they are sleeping and dreaming. However, it doesn't look peaceful when this happens. The dog might also evacuate their bowels and/or bladder when they are suffering from a seizure.

Other dogs might have a dazed look on their face during the seizure. They might seem confused or unsteady. You might also notice the dog looking off into space blankly before they suffer from a seizure.

After the seizures occur, it is common for the dog to seem disoriented and confused. They might even seem temporarily blind. You might see the dog walking in circles and bumping into things, not seeming to understand where they are or where they are going. Because there is a potential for them to bite their own tongue or lips, you might even see bleeding from the mouth.

Strangely, the dog might also try to hide after they've gone through a seizure. This could be because they are confused or could be because they do not want others to see what they may perceive as a weakness.

Keep the Dog Safe

When the dog is going through the seizure, it is natural for you to want to make sure they are safe. However, you have to do this in a way that manages to not only keep the dog safe, but also keep *you* safe. This is especially true if you have a large dog, though you need to be just as careful with a smaller dog.

Don't Lose Your Fingers

While many people believe that a dog will swallow their tongue if they are going through a seizure, it's not true. They won't. If you attempt to put your fingers into your dog's mouth to keep them from swallowing their tongue, you run a good chance of being bitten badly. You'd also injure the dog if you try to do this. If you have a particularly large dog, you could lose part of a finger. Even a smaller dog's teeth can do a lot of damage.

They don't mean to bite, but they don't have any control when they're going through the seizure.

Keeping the Dog from Hurting Itself

The best thing you can do to keep the dog from hurting itself is to make sure they are not going to knock into items in the room. Keep the space as clear as you can and move items out of the way. They will be safer once they are on the floor or on the ground. Make sure that you stay with the dog until the seizure passes and observe them afterwards.

Having a single seizure is rarely going to be a danger for the dog. However, if the dog is suffering from multiple seizures in a short period, also called cluster seizures, it could be a major problem. The same is true if the seizure they suffer lasts for longer than a few minutes.

You will also want to keep an eye on the temperature of the dog. If they are suffering from hyperthermia, which is an elevated body temperature, after the seizure, it is time to talk with the vet.

In addition, a condition known as a status epilepticus is extremely dangerous to the dog. This is a seizure that lasts for more than five minutes. If this occurs, you need to take the dog to the vet right away. If it happens overnight, you need to find an emergency vet.

What Happens Next?

After the dog has suffered a seizure, you will speak with your vet, and they will try to get to the bottom of just why the seizure occurred. If the dog does not have more than one seizure a month, then they might not recommend any type of treatment at all.

However, if they have more than one seizure a month, if they suffered from cluster seizures or if they had seizures that were severe or prolonged, they will begin some type of treatment.

Medication as Treatment

Treatment is typically in the form of medication. There are several common medications used to treat dogs experiencing seizures. These include potassium bromide, phenobarbital, felbamate, zonisamind, levetiracetam, and gabapentin.

After starting the anticonvulsant medication, it needs to be given to the dog for the rest of their life. This is because evidence has shown that if the medication is discontinued, the dog could have a greater risk of developing seizures that are even *more* severe in the future.

You can talk with your vet about the best medications to try and how to put the dog on a schedule to make sure they are taking the proper meds.

Keep in mind that even though medications for seizures might be able to reduce the risk of seizures, there is no cure, and there is still a chance that seizures could occasionally occur.

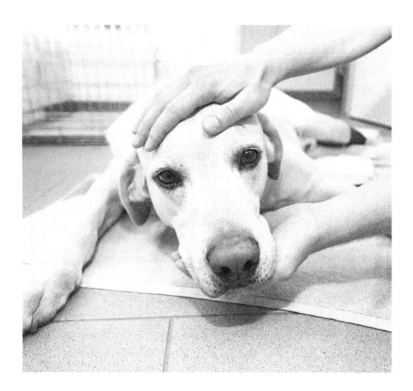

Chapter 6: Canine Cancer

Cancer is an insidious disease that can affect your dog, just as it can affect the humans that you love. In fact, cancer happens to be the leading cause of death in dogs over the age of 10. However, half of all cancers are able to be properly treated if they are caught in time.

Diagnosis

It is important for you to be familiar with some of the potential symptoms that could indicate that your dog is suffering from health problems such as cancer. For example, you will want to look for lumps on the skin and changes to the skin texture or appearance that look odd. You will also want to pay attention to unexpected weight loss, as this is a common symptom in canine cancer.

Other potential symptoms include difficulties breathing, coughing, wounds that won't heal, changes in the dog's behavior, or an inability to control their bladder or bowels that might indicate that they have cancer. However, none of these are 100%, surefire signs of cancer.

You may have noticed that there tends to be some similarities between these types of symptoms and other health conditions that the dog might be dealing with other than cancer. You will not be able to tell that your dog has cancer simply by observing them. You will need to *take your dog to the vet, so they can be tested properly.*

Types of Cancer in Dogs

According to veterinary oncologists, around 50% of dogs over 10 years old will develop cancer at some point. There are many different types of cancer that can develop in dogs including malignant lymphoma, skin cancer, breast cancer, and soft tissue sarcomas. Let's take a closer look at some of these types of cancers.

Lymphoma

This is a term used for malignant neoplastic disorders of the lymph tissue. This tends to be the most commonly treated type of systemic cancer by vets today. This type of cancer tends to be quite aggressive. However, if it is diagnosed early enough, it is possible to manage it. Without treatment, it typically leads to death.

Many times, this will involve more than one lymph node. It can involve the spleen, liver, as well as other organs. During the latter stages of the disease, it is common for bone marrow to become cancerous, as well.

Oral Cancer

Tumors can affect the mouth and throat of dogs, as well. The most common of these tumors is a malignant melanoma.

However, there are others, such as squamous cell carcinoma and fibrosarcoma. Typically, the tumors are biopsied and the dog will be given an x-ray or a CT scan. This will help to determine how extensive the disease has become.

A common course of treatment is surgical removal. In some cases, radiation therapy and treatment can help, as well.

Hemangiosarcoma

This is a malignant type of cancer that is metastatic. It starts from the cells that line the blood vessels. This can affect many areas of the dog's body, including the spleen, skin, liver, and heart. However, it has the potential to spread anywhere. The type of treatment that is typically utilized is surgery to remove the cancer.

Osteosarcoma

This is a type of malignant neoplasia and the most common type of bone cancer in dogs. It will involve increases in the amount of bone being produced, and it typically happens with larger breeds of dogs that are middle-aged to older. It affects both male and female dogs.

This is a very aggressive type of cancer. It will typically be presented through lameness in older, larger dogs. This lameness will get worse over time, and in some cases, there might even be swelling at the site of the tumor.

The most common treatment for this type of cancer is surgical removal through amputation. The amputation, in addition to the chemotherapy, can help to improve the dog's quality of life.

Mammary Cancer

Tumors in the mammary glands are the most common types of tumors that affect female dogs that have not been spayed. In fact, about 50% of the tumors in female dogs are from mammary tumors. It is more common in dogs older than nine years old and that have not been spayed or that were not spayed until they went through their second heat cycle. When this type of cancer is diagnosed early enough, surgical treatment tends to be the most common choice. In addition, the vet might recommend that the dog goes through chemotherapy, as well.

Soft Tissue Sarcoma

There different types of sarcomas included under this umbrella term. Some of these include nerve sheath tumors, malignant fibrous histiocytoma, fibrosarcoma, neurofibrosarcoma, liposarcoma, and hemangiopericytoma.

These types of tumors tend to be more common in dogs in their middle to older ages, and they are also more common in larger breeds. These types of sarcomas tend to show up without warning and they will appear as a mass located on or under the skin. Often, they will appear near the chest, legs, or mouth. These are typically taken care of by surgery, although the vet will determine what options will work best for dealing with the cancer.

Mast Cell Tumors

These types of tumors will often start as skin tumors. The mast cells can eventually release substances that cause other issues, such as ulcers in the stomach and lesions on the skin. These types of tumors can become malignant, and whenever they are seen, they should be treated quickly.

Some of the treatment options that could work for these types of tumors include surgery, radiation, and chemotherapy. The treatment that is chosen will be determined by the vet's recommendations, and they will generally depend on the stage of the tumor.

Choosing Treatments

When it comes to the types of treatments that you should choose for your dog's cancer, the decision is typically made for you by the type of cancer the dog develops. For bone cancer in the leg, for example, amputation and chemotherapy are common because they offer the best potential for survival.

You will find that the best treatment for you to choose is not always the treatment that you initially want. You need to consider a range of factors along with your vet when you are making your decision. Consider the health of your dog currently, the type of cancer, and the treatments that work best for that type of cancer.

Still, it's a good idea to have some knowledge about what the common types of treatment are for the dogs and what you can expect. Then, we'll discuss some of the less conventional treatments, including supplements and lifestyle changes that may be able to help.

Surgery

In some cases, the best and most effective method for treating cancer in canines is surgery. The goal of surgery is to remove or reduce the main cancerous tumors. In some cases, it might be possible to remove most or all of the cancer. However, this type of treatment is typically combined with either chemotherapy or radiation therapy to be more effective.

Before your pet undergoes any surgery, the veterinarian will run tests to make sure they are healthy enough to go through the surgery. There are different types of surgery that are done based on the type of cancer. For example, as already mentioned, if a dog suffers from bone cancer, amputating the limb might be the best option for them. With other types of cancer, it might be possible for surgical removal of the entire tumor, thus removing all of the cancer.

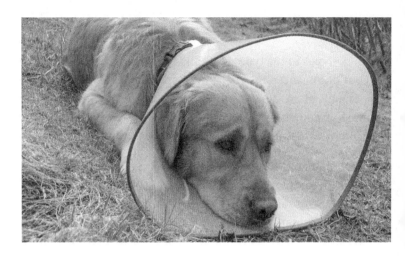

The side effects of the surgery can vary, but you'll find that many dogs will be in pain, particularly at the surgical site. The veterinarian will provide medicine that can help to relieve the dog's pain. The dog will want to take it easy after undergoing surgery.

Chemotherapy

Another common treatment recommended by veterinarian oncologists to treat cancer is chemotherapy. The goal is always to provide a good quality of life for the dog. In some cases, chemotherapy might be the only treatment used to deal with the cancer. Other times, it might be used in conjunction with other types of treatment, such as surgery and radiation therapy.

Typically, this type of treatment will be utilized for cancer that has already spread to other areas of the body. It could also be used for tumors that are occurring in more than one area of the body, or for those that are too large or difficult to remove surgically. In some instances, it might even be able to shrink large tumors to the point where they can be removed surgically.

The two most common methods of administering chemotherapy are through intravenous methods or orally. When a dog goes through this type of treatment, they are typically given other supportive medications, that can help them deal with some of the side effects, such as nausea, diarrhea, and the like. As your dog undergoes chemotherapy, you may also notice that they tend to be a bit more tired than they typically are.

Chemotherapy is a common treatment for osteosarcoma, lymphoma, hemangiosarcoma, mast cell tumors, mammary gland tumors, and different types of gastrointestinal tumors. The vet will help you determine whether this is the best treatment for your dog.

Radiation

Radiation therapy is another treatment that can be used for canine cancer. Typically, this is used after surgery or in conjunction with chemotherapy and other targeted therapies. The goal of radiation therapy is to eliminate any further cancer cells that could remain following the surgery or chemo. By killing the remaining and potentially cancerous cells, it can help to reduce the risk of the cancer returning.

In addition, radiation therapy has even been used to help ease the pain of certain cancers in dogs, including bone cancer. This is called palliative radiation therapy.

In a veterinary setting, radiation therapy is typically delivered using a linear accelerator. It will deliver ionizing radiation to the cancer cells, which help to ensure that they do not divide and grow. It is important to keep in mind that both normal and cancerous cells are affected. This type of therapy is given over a course of several treatments.

Side Effects

As with humans, there are a range of side effects that can occur when radiation therapy is provided. One of the common effects include hair loss at the site that has been irradiated. In some cases, the dog might suffer from diarrhea, vomiting, nausea, and a decreased appetite. The side effects are typically resolved quickly, but if they are not, you can speak with your veterinarian.

Supplements for Treatment

There aren't truly any supplements that will help to treat the cancer itself, of course. However, there are a number of supplements that can help to manage some symptoms from the cancer and the side effects of the cancer treatments.

- Ginger
- Glutamine
- Apocaps
- Neoplasene
- Beta glucans
- Fish oil
- Artemisinin
- CBD oil

Lifestyle

You will find that making some lifestyle changes, namely to the dog's exercise and diet, is important when it comes to their treatment and to help keep the dog more comfortable.

Exercise

Dogs that have cancer will often have more problems with their mobility. They will not be able to exercise and move as easily as they once did, and this will typically mean that their exercise routine will need to change. In most cases, it will mean that they need to take it slow. They might even need to use a doggie wheelchair like those mentioned earlier.

Keep the walks short and give the dog plenty of time to rest. It can take them a long time to heal from various types of treatment, and the cancer itself can be exhausting to the dog.

Diet

Having a healthy diet that is full of vitamins, antioxidants, and omega-3 fatty acids is important through all stages of a dog's life whether they are healthy or ill. When they are suffering from cancer and going through treatment, this is especially important. They will not be able to always get the nutrients they need through a typical store-bought pet food. You will want to consider switching the food to a more natural and vitamin-rich diet, and perhaps even making your own dog food, if you have not already.

Cancer Prevention Tips

While there may not be any 100% workable methods that will prevent your dog from getting cancer, there are still some things that you can do to help reduce the risks they are facing. Let's look at some of the things that can be done.

It is a good idea to spay the dog. If you spay her before she goes into her first heat, it reduces the chance of mammary cancer substantially.

In addition, providing good oral care for the dog can help to reduce the risk of oral cancers.

When first choosing a dog, learn more about the breed if to see if it is more prone to suffering from cancer. Some of the breeds that have the highest cancer rate include:

- Rottweiler
- Bernese Mountain Dog
- Bouvier des Flandres
- German Shepherd
- Great Dane
- Labrador Retriever
- Bichon Frise

- Boxer
- Golden Retriever

Provide your dog with a quality diet and plenty of exercise and be sure to take them to the vet for regular checkups. This helps to catch cancers early, so they have a better chance of being treated.

However, it is important to remember that prevention is quite difficult because people are still not entirely certain of the cause of most canine cancers. While finding ways of prevention is important, it is also highly important to treat it as early as possible if you want the best results.

Chapter 7: Canine Heart Disease

Heart disease is unfortunately common in dogs. Dogs who suffer from heart disease and heart failure could tire more easily than other dogs, and easier than they once did. You might notice a lack of appetite, as well. You may also notice the dog coughs. Of course, there are also signs and symptoms of a number of other potential canine maladies.

Therefore, it is important to have a better understanding of this disease, the causes, diagnosis, and treatment.

The Signs of Canine Heart Disease

Having early diagnosis and treatment can make a major difference when it comes to heart disease in dogs.

- *Coughing* – While coughing is a common symptom of a wide range of illnesses, one of those illnesses is heart disease. A minor cough will typically only last a couple of days. However, if you notice that your dog is still coughing after three days or that they have other symptoms, you will want to seek veterinary care.

- *Difficulty Breathing* - You might also notice that the dog has difficulty breathing. The breathing might seem labored or they might be short of breath. You might also notice that they have rapid breathing, even when they have not exerted themselves. This could also be an indicator of heart disease.

- *Behavior Changes* – Does the dog seem as playful as usual? Do they seem more reluctant to get out and exercise? Do they not want to be as affectionate? These are signs of heart disease.

- *Changes in Weight* – If you notice a change in the weight of the dog, either up or down, it could be a sign of a health problem, including heart disease.

- *Poor Appetite* – Along the same lines, if the dog does not have an appetite, it typically means that something is wrong. When this is combined with other elements on this list, it could be a good indicator of heart disease.

- *Weakness* - A dog that shows physical weakness could just be a general indicator of them getting older. However, it could be more serious. If the weakness is combined with other problems on this list, it could be a sign of heart disease, and you should seek attention from your vet.

- *Restlessness* – If you notice that your dog tends to be restless at night, there is the potential that it could be an indicator.

- *Isolation* – Does your dog want less to do with you? Are they isolating themselves from you, your family, or other pets? There is a chance that this could mean heart disease.

- *Edema* – This is the swelling of tissues in the body. If you notice that there is swelling in the limbs or abdomen, it could be a sign that they have heart disease.

- *Fainting or Collapsing* – Whenever your dog collapses or faints, you should see the vet. It could be an indicator of many different types of health problems, and one of those issues is heart disease.

Getting a Diagnosis

As you have probably noticed, many of the signs and symptoms of potential heart disease in your dog are similar to a wide range of other health problems the dog might be facing. Heart disease, like so many other of these terrible ailments, is not something you will be able to diagnose on your own. You need to take your dog to the vet to find out exactly what is wrong with them.

What Causes Heart Disease in Dogs?

There are two types of heart disease in dogs. These are *congenital* and *acquired*.

When it comes to congenital heart disease, this is something that is present at the birth of the dog, and that might've been inherited from the dog's parents. The types of issues that can occur with the heart in this case can vary, but they are all serious.

With acquired heart disease, the problem can occur for a wide range of reasons. This type of heart disease typically affects dogs in their middle to senior years, and the disease develops over time. Some of the common types of dog heart disease include arrhythmias, pericardial disease, mitral valve disease, and chronic valvular heart disease.

Let's take a closer look at some of these causes of acquired heart disease.

Valvular disease, which can damage the mitral valve, is common in small breed dogs.

Myocardial diseases can affect the muscles of the heart, and these tend to be more common in larger dogs.

Injuries and infections to the heart can increase the risk of acquiring disease. Some of the types of infections that could increase the risk include the parvovirus infection and heart worm.

These are some of the potential problems that can cause heart disease in dogs. All of these can be quite serious, so you need to get the advice of your veterinarian when it comes to treatment.

The Treatment

Your veterinarian will be able to let you know about various types of drugs that can be used to treat heart disease in dogs. The medication will be chosen based on the type of heart disease that the dog has, as well as the overall health of the animal and the severity of the heart disease.

Keep in mind that there are no cures for heart disease and heart failure in dogs. However with the proper treatment, it is possible for them to live a number of years after they have been diagnosed.

A dog that suffers from heart disease requires special care and monitoring while they're at home. You will need to make sure they are receiving their medication at the right times, and you need to keep a close eye on them to see if their condition worsens.

Chapter 8: Canine Kidney Disease

Another disease that tends to affect a large number of dogs is kidney disease. A dog's kidneys work in much the same way as your kidneys. They are used for filtering waste from the blood. They help to maintain normal concentrations of water and salt in the body and they help control blood pressure. They serve a wide range of functions in the body, and when something is wrong with them, the person, or dog in this case, becomes ill.

What Causes the Kidney Problems?

Suffering from *acute kidney failure* can result from a range of reasons. It can affect both young and old dogs, as it can occur because of the ingestion of toxins, tainted food, and certain types of medications. Of course, as a dog gets older, kidney problems can develop because of a reduced blood flow to the kidneys, infections, obstructions in the urinary tract, and other factors.

Chronic kidney disease will typically show up over a longer period of time, and the causes can be difficult to determine. This is the type of the issue that seems to affect older dogs more often. This will typically be caused by some underlying illness. It could also be due to hereditary conditions.

Interestingly, one of the main causes of chronic kidney failure in dogs is dental disease. This is one of the reasons it is so important to make sure that you provide your dog with good dental care throughout their life. Bacteria that gets into the blood because of dental disease can cause serious damage to the kidneys, as well as to the liver and heart.

What Are Symptoms of Kidney Problems in Dogs

There are different signs and symptoms that could indicate a dog is having some type of kidney problems. The most common include:

- Change in water consumption
- Change in the amount of urine produced
- Depression
- Loss of appetite
- Vomiting
- Weight loss
- Blood and urine
- Mouth ulcers
- Pale gums
- A chemical odor on the breath
- Stumbling

Any of these could be an indicator of kidney problems or kidney disease, as well as other canine illnesses. If you notice that your dog is suffering from any of these issues, it is in your best interest to take them to the vet.

Prevention of Kidney Problems

Some types of kidney problems can't really be prevented, as they could be hereditary. However, other types of issues with the kidneys can certainly be prevented. You will want to make sure that you ensure your dog never has access to substances that could be dangerous and toxic to them. Never give the dog over the counter medications without being instructed to do so by your vet. Also, make sure that your dog has access to water all the time. As mentioned, oral hygiene is also extremely important. In addition, provide your dog with a healthy diet.

Treatment for Kidney Issues

Before the vet is able to treat kidney disease, they need to find out what caused it. Therefore, as usual, you need an evaluation from the vet.

One of the common types of treatment during the early stages of kidney disease is known as fluid therapy. The veterinarian will administer fluids intravenously to the dog over an extended period. The amount of time it takes can vary from one dog to another based on their size, naturally.

During this time, the dog will be monitored to make sure they urinate properly. In some cases, the veterinarian may need to provide medication along with IV fluids in order to help the dog urinate.

If fluid therapy is not enough, the dog may undergo kidney dialysis similar to what a human goes through. This type of treatment can also be helpful for dogs who have taken toxins into their body or those who have suffered trauma that affected their urinary tract.

There are options for kidney transplants, as well. However, it is important to note that these are only available in certain animal hospitals, and these procedures do tend to be rather costly.

Diet and Supplementation Could Help

It is possible to help a dog suffering from kidney problems by improving their diet. Typically, dogs are supposed to have a high-protein diet. However, when they have kidney problems, they need to switch to a low-protein diet. This is easier on the kidneys. You will want to watch sodium intake and make sure they are also eating a low phosphorus diet.

Additionally, avoid serving dry food that's low on water. Balance the diet by offering both moist and dry foods. Always make sure the dog has plenty to drink.

You can also find that some supplements and vitamins could be helpful for the dog who is suffering from kidney problems. Many of these are items already suggested for a healthy canine diet. These include omega-3 fatty acids, water-soluble B and C vitamins, moderate amounts of vitamin A and vitamin D, and phosphate binders. In addition, the vet might want you to provide the dog with a kidney glandular supplement.

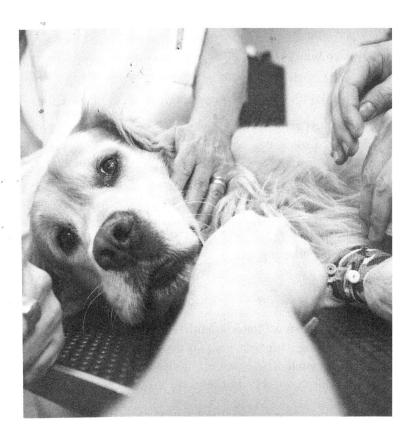

Chapter 9: Is It an Emergency?

When you have an older dog, it can often feel like every little thing that happens with the dog is a serious emergency. Everything that happens makes you believe that you need to rush to the vet, and if your vet isn't open, that you need to head to an emergency vet. While having this amount of attention and care for your pet is certainly admirable, it doesn't always mean that you are dealing with a true emergency.

You will want to know whether your dog is suffering from a condition that is a true emergency before you rush to the animal ER. The following are emergency symptoms that will require that you take your dog to the vet right away.

- Open wounds
- Broken bones
- Trauma, such as being hit by a car
- Breathing stopped, or the dog suddenly went unconscious
- Vomiting blood
- Repeated vomiting
- Seizure
- Sudden collapse
- Difficulty breathing
- Bleeding from the mouth, nose, or eyes
- Possible poisoning
- Extreme pain
- Hard and swollen abdomen

These are all serious conditions that mean there is something seriously wrong with your pet that needs to be taken care of as quickly as possible. These are not conditions that you will want to "wait out" for the weekend to see if the dog gets better.

Of course, most people have the opposite problem. They believe that every little cough and every time the dog seems tired means that they need to rush them to the vet for help. Unless it is a true emergency, as noted above, then it can probably wait until the next day.

Chapter 10: About You

Thus far, we've talked about what you need to do to help make your dog's life better during this time. Even though your senior dog with health problems is certainly going through a lot at this time, so are you.

After all, you are the one who is constantly worried about your canine friend. You are the one who is making sure that they have their medications on time, that they get to their vet appointments, and that they are as comfortable as they can be. You are the one who is up for hours at night reading online about new treatments for your dog's conditions.

It has the potential to take quite a toll on you, and you need to make sure that you are taking proper care of yourself. It is imperative that you find ways that you can still get the rest you need so you can enjoy life in the time that you have with your pet, not to mention the rest of your family.

Empathy and Coping with Sorrow

It is important that you have at least one other person around you that can empathize with what you are feeling and the sorrow that you have regarding your dog's condition and declining health. If you are fortunate, you will have family members that understand what you are going through, and who can help out with some of the tasks of caring for the dog.

In addition, even though you still have your pet with you at this point, it is entirely natural that you are feeling a substantial amount of sorrow. You know what's coming in the near future, and you might not be ready to say goodbye quite yet. This means that in between the work you are putting into taking care of your dog, you might suffer from bouts of sorrow.

If you are not careful, you can let this sorrow get the better of you. It could end up keeping you sad and even isolated from your family and friends. It is important that you learn to understand the sorrow and cope with it as best you can.

In the final chapter, we will be looking more closely at grief, which is tied closely to sorrow. However, at this point, when your dog is still with you, you are likely feeling sorrow for the plight of your animal. You want to do everything you can to make their life as happy and cushy as it can possibly be right now, and that's a good thing.

However, you can't let your own health or sanity suffer.

Getting Enough Sleep

Sometimes, it is difficult to provide your dog with all of the care that they need, and still take care of yourself. You still need to eat, and you still need to make sure you are getting plenty of sleep. If you don't, it will affect other aspects of your life, including your work and your social life.

If you have a dog that requires medication at regular intervals, for example, you might want to trade off who is getting up to provide them medication through the night. You could even hire someone to handle it for you if you can't do it on your own.

Having a Plan

The best way to make sure you can take care of both the dog and yourself is to have a plan in place. You can work with your veterinarian to get a better idea of how to develop a plan to help with their medical needs, feeding, exercise, and more. Different dogs will, of course, have different types of illnesses and needs, and the schedule will vary from one dog to another. There is no single plan that will work for everyone.

In addition, you need to make sure that your plans are flexible. You never know when the dog might need some extra attention or help. There is also the chance that other ailments with the dog could cause changes to the plan.

Keeping Records and Notes

It is always a good idea to keep track of everything that you are doing for the dog. Note when they are getting their medications, and how they are behaving after they have taken the meds, for example. This will let you know if there is an unexpected side effect or change in behavior that could be due to the medicine. Keep track of how the dog seems to feel, whether they are more lethargic or more energetic, whether they are sleeping or not, etc.

The better your notes the better the vet will be able to provide treatments and care for your dog.

Planning for the Future

In addition to having a schedule and a plan for yourself and your dog right now, you will also need to make sure that you are planning for the future and what will happen. Even with all of the best treatments in the world, dogs will not live forever. There will come a time when it is in their best interest to let them go, and that's what we will be covering next.

Chapter 11: End of Life

This is a difficult chapter to read, to be sure. It is the last chapter, appropriately, and it is very important for those who have dogs that are nearing their own last chapter.

The View of Death

Humans and animals both want to live. The fight for survival is natural amongst anything that is living. However, actual perspectives on death will vary substantially from humans to animals. Your dog only knows that she's not feeling well and that she has some problems making it outside. She knows that she's in pain, and she doesn't like that.

However, she doesn't fear death because she doesn't have a concept of it, at least not the same way that humans do. Yes, she wants to live... she wants to go on doing the same things that she's always done, as she knows nothing else.

Humans have a very different view of death. Many dread and fear it whether it is their own death or the death of a loved one. They see it as the end, and they don't want things to end. Dogs are fortunate in the fact that they really don't have a concept of an end, and they tend not to be worried about death.

You should take this as comforting. It means that she won't have a fear of death as it comes for her. It means that you can be with her and comfort her right up until the end of her life. It will hurt you, but it will bring her peace.

Animal Pain

Animals feel pain. This should be obvious to anyone who has been around an animal for any length of time. When a cat's tail is mistakenly clipped by a closing screen door, the animal let's out a yell of shock and pain. When your dog is in pain, you can see it. They feel pain just as acutely as people do. After all, they have blood and bones and nerves just like people do. Anyone who says that your dog doesn't feel pain is not being honest with themselves.

When a dog is near the end of their life, and they are suffering from conditions like those mentioned in this book, they are likely in pain. This means that their quality of life has diminished substantially. They feel pain that is with them almost constantly, and even medications do not always help.

In these cases, it typically means that you will want to consider the next step, which is euthanasia.

Euthanasia

You have spent a long time bonding with your dog over the years, and the last thing that you can imagine is being the one who makes the decision about when they should die. However, even though that's typically what many people think about when it comes to euthanasia, that's not the way you should look at it. Your dog, your *friend*, is in a substantial amount of pain. Euthanasia can help to end that pain.

When Is It Time?

When you see that your dog is in pain, and that her quality of life has suffered so much that she's only a shell of what she was before, you know that it's time for euthanasia. If the dog is not eating and drinking, if they have lost the desire to be around people, and if they are not responding to treatments any longer, it is time.

You might want to get a second opinion from another vet, but they are likely to tell you the same thing and that there are no other treatments that will help her get better, euthanasia is the right choice. If you notice that she's suffering, and you can't stand to see her keep going through all of that pain, then you know that it's the right time.

Resources for Making a Last Decision

Making this type of decision will never be easy, and you will want to utilize some resources to help you make your decision. One of the best resources, of course, is speaking with your vet. They have seen other dogs in the same or similar situations before whose owners may have waited for euthanasia. They can help to guide you along the right path. You might also want to talk with adult family members and friends, as well. You can also find online resources through the Humane Society.

Last Day with Your Friend

Depending on how far gone the dog is at this point, your last day with her can vary. You want to make her day as special and as pleasant as possible. Give her any treats that you know she loves, as much as she wants, if she's still eating. Take her to her favorite spots if she's able to get out and spend time with her. Talk with her gently, and make sure she has all of her favorite things nearby. The goal is to make her day one that you will remember.

Before, During, and After – What to Expect

You have the choice to be with your pet during the euthanasia procedure when the solution is administered by the veterinarian. There are some who can't imaging being in the same room when their dog passes away, and there are others who can't imagine *not* being with their friend during their final moments. It is important that you take some time to think this through and weigh the pros and cons of each.

While it is ultimately your decision, you don't want to later regret *not* being there in the final moments. It is normal to be sad and to cry, and the vet expects this. You don't have to hold back.

The Procedure

The veterinarian will administer the solution intravenously. In some cases, the vet will need to sedate the pet to make sure that they are calm enough to have the IV placed into them for the solution. It will depend on the dog whether sedation should be administered, and this is something that you can talk about with your vet before the appointment.

Once the solution has been administered, it goes to work quickly, providing your pet with a peaceful, painless and humane death. Once the solution has entered the bloodstream of the dog, it will take about 10 seconds before the dog takes a breath. They grow weaker, and they appear to go to sleep. They will then likely take several more breaths before the dog is truly gone.

You may want to hold your dog during the procedure, and that should not be a problem at all.

Living with the Decision

When you make the decision to euthanize your pet, it can bring a heaping dose of guilt along with it, even though you know that you made the right decision. You feel as if it was somehow you who were at fault for making time pass and your dog get older, or that it was your fault they got cancer. In the beginning, many people find that they have a hard time living with the decision, but with a little bit of space, they do realize that they made the right decision. They have made sure that their friend is no longer ill and in pain. Still, that doesn't mean that the grief goes away immediately.

Dealing With Grief

You didn't just lose a pet or your dog. You lost a friend, a part of your family who was a constant companion in your life for a long time. They brought fun, joy, and happiness to you, and now that they are gone, it is normal for you to feel grief just as strongly as if you had lost any other friend. It is important to understand the stages of grief and what you can expect as you work your way through them.

Stages of Grief

People will typically go through five stages of grief after their dog has died. These grief stages are exactly the same as if they had lost a human. It takes different people different amounts of time to make it through each of the five stages, and you should never try to rush it.

The five stages of grief include:
- Denial
- Anger
- Bargaining
- Depression
- Acceptance

Work your way through the loss of your dog as best you can, understanding that other members of your family or friend group will go through the process in their own way. This means that they might proceed faster or slower through the stages of grief than you do.

Resources

You likely have some resources that can help you with your grief. These could be your family members and friends, along with other pets that still need you to be there and care for them. In addition, you will find online support groups for those who have lost pets, such as PetLoss.com. Some humane societies and veterinarian clinics might also have support groups and materials to help you during this time. Talk with your vet to see if they have any suggestions.

Beyond the Grief

Eventually, the grief will leave. This doesn't mean that you forget your dog by any means, but it means that you are feeling better. You are getting to the point where you can move on with your life without everything reminding you of your dog. You can look back at your photos and videos of the dog fondly and enjoy those great memories without bursting into tears. Of course, this doesn't mean that the sadness is banished forever. There may still be those times when you get a little sad and wistful when you think about your departed canine companion.

Eventually, you might find that you are at a point where you want to bring a new dog into your life. This can be a great addition to the family, but it is important to make sure that you are treating the new dog as a unique little boy or girl rather than thinking that they will be just like your old dog.

Remembering Your Dog

Even if you do eventually get another dog, you probably want to find some ways that you can remember the best friend that you just lost. They are gone, but they are not forgotten. Fortunately, there are a number of things you can do that will help you with this.

First, you could get your pet's ashes to place in an urn. You could scatter these ashes in their favorite places, or you could put them on the mantle. If the pet was not cremated, you could have buried them at home or in a pet cemetery. Visiting the grave can provide you with a sense of still being near your pet. Perhaps you want to commission a custom piece of art, such as a painting of your pet.

Of course, you will also want to look at the collection of photos and videos that you have of your pet from time to time. This will provide you with a happy and warm feeling as you remember your furry little friend and all the joy that they brought to you.

There are plenty of things you can do to help you remember your pet. They might be gone, but that does not mean that you forget them.

Conclusion

With the information and the tips that have been provided in this book, you will have a better understanding of just what your senior dog is going through in their later years.

You should be able to have a deeper knowledge of the types of aches and pains they feel, some of the most common conditions with them, and some of the issues they suffer as they are going through cognitive decline.

It's not possible to rationalize with a dog. You can't talk to them and let them know what's happening and why they are feeling the way they do. As smart as your dog might be, they can't understand things like cancer or joint problems. They just know that things aren't quite what they used to be and maybe they feel sick. It's your duty to be there for them, not as an owner, but as a companion.

Your Love Won't Diminish When They're Gone

Your dog is not merely a pet. When people say that their dog is a member of the family, it's not just hyperbole.

You've been together for years, through thick and thin, and they've never let you down. They've always been on your side and had your back. When you've been sad and down, they've been there. When you've been happy, they've been wagging their tail right along with you.

Going through the last stages of their life with them can be difficult, but the ultimate goal of this book is to provide you with the knowledge you need to make it as easy as possible for them.

With the knowledge from the book, and help from your vet, you can work to provide a comfortable environment for them and make their senior years and final days as happy as they can possibly be.

You can be with them right up to the end, which is just as it should be. Stay strong and keep hold of all of those good memories.

Resources

https://pets.webmd.com/dogs/how-to-calculate-your-dogs-age
https://www.dogingtonpost.com/is-your-old-dog-drinking-water-excessively/
https://www.wisegeek.com/what-are-some-reasons-why-my-dog-is-not-drinking-water.htm
https://www.petful.com/pet-health/help-sick-pet-wont-eat/
http://talesandtails.com/what-ive-learned-about-getting-old-dogs-to-eat/
https://yourolddog.com/how-to-get-your-older-dog-to-eat/
https://www.petmd.com/dog/general-health/incontinence-senior-dogs-what-do-and-how-help
https://pets.webmd.com/dogs/guide/behavior-problems-older-dogs#1
https://www.petcarerx.com/article/10-symptoms-in-older-dogs-you-shouldnt-ignore/595
https://www.petmd.com/dog/grooming/evr_dg_oral_hygiene_and_your_dogs_health
https://www.natural-dog-health-remedies.com/canine-insomnia.html
https://www.dogshealth.com/blog/why-dogs-sleep-so-much/
https://www.cuteness.com/article/causes-dogs-sleeping-much
https://www.petmd.com/dog/wellness/evr_dg_exercise_for_your_senior_do
https://www.petmd.com/dog/care/evr_dg_caring_for_older_dogs_with_health_problems
https://www.preventivevet.com/dogs/how-to-help-an-older-dog-with-arthritis-and-other-mobility-issues
https://www.dummies.com/pets/dogs/handling-the-problems-of-old-age-in-your-dog/
http://www.vetstreet.com/our-pet-experts/10-life-improving-products-for-senior-dogs
https://www.k9ofmine.com/older-dog-incontinence/
http://www.vetstreet.com/our-pet-experts/7-products-to-help-senior-or-disabled-dogs-get-back-on-their-paws
https://www.petdoors.com/keeping-out-raccoons.html
https://www.puplife.com/pages/how-to-choose-the-right-dog-bed
http://www.vetstreet.com/our-pet-experts/how-to-choose-the-perfect-bed-for-your-dog
https://www.orvis.com/how-to-choose-a-dog-bed-a-comprehensive-guide
https://www.dog.com/content/Senior-Dogs/Choosing-The-Right-Bed-For-The-Senior-Dog/
https://www.k9ofmine.com/best-dog-beds-for-arthritic-dogs/
https://www.overstock.com/guides/how-to-choose-a-pet-bed-for-an-older-dog
https://iheartdogs.com/how-to-choose-a-bed-for-your-senior-dog-help-him-get-the-best-rest-possible/
https://www.petlovesbest.com/how-to-choose-a-dog-bed/
http://philosophyofdog.com/6-alternative-treatment-options-for-senior-dogs/
https://www.nomnomnow.com/learn/pet-nutrition/senior-dog-food-guide
https://www.dummies.com/pets/dogs/adapting-the-environment-for-your-senior-dog/
https://flexpet.com/5-tips-for-living-with-a-senior-dog/
https://pets.webmd.com/dogs/guide/dog-joint-health-pain-osteoarthritis-and-other-joint-problems#1
https://topdogtips.com/joint-pain-in-dogs-signs/
https://www.akc.org/expert-advice/health/dealing-with-canine-arthritis/
https://www.petcarerx.com/article/8-ways-to-treat-dog-joint-pain/1403
https://www.wisegeek.com/what-are-the-signs-of-joint-pain-in-dogs.htm
https://www.thesprucepets.com/guide-to-pain-medications-for-dogs-189671
https://www.vetinfo.com/dog-arthritis-medications.html
https://www.fda.gov/AnimalVeterinary/ResourcesforYou/AnimalHealthLiteracy/ucm392732.htm#Effects
https://topdogtips.com/best-dog-arthritis-supplements/
https://www.dogsbynina.com/best-3-joint-supplements-for-dogs/
https://www.caninearthritisandjoint.com/how-to-massage-your-dog.html
https://dogquality.com/blogs/senior-dog-blog/59698627-prosthetics-improving-mobility-for-dog-amputees
https://www.handicappedpets.com/k9-dog-orthotics-prosthetics/
https://topdogtips.com/arthritis-diet-for-dogs/
https://www.wikihow.com/Recognize-Signs-of-Anxiety-in-Dogs
https://thebark.com/content/should-you-treat-your-dog-stem-cell-therapy
https://pathwithpaws.com/blog/2010/02/01/dementia-and-anxiety-in-your-older-dog-what-to-do/
https://www.petcarerx.com/article/how-to-know-if-your-dog-has-anxiety/702
https://wagwalking.com/condition/dementia-geriatric
https://www.rover.com/blog/canine-cognitive-dysfunction-major-symptoms/
https://dogdementia.com/canine-cognitive-dysfunction-what-you-need-to-know/
https://www.petmd.com/dog/slideshows/care/common-ailments-for-senior-dogs
https://www.thesprucepets.com/senior-dog-health-3385021
https://pets.webmd.com/dogs/dog-seizure-disorders#1
https://vcahospitals.com/know-your-pet/seizures-general-for-dogs
https://www.thesprucepets.com/anti-convulsant-medications-3384864
https://healthquestions.medhelp.org/seizure-in-geriatric-dog
https://pets.webmd.com/dogs/guide/dogs-and-cancer-get-the-facts#1
https://www.petmd.com/dog/slideshows/general-health/dog-breeds-highest-cancer-rate
https://www.petwave.com/Dogs/Health/Cancer/Types.aspx
https://www.dogzhealth.com/cancer-treatment-for-dog/
https://www.dogcancerblog.com/articles/full-spectrum-cancer-care/nutraceuticals/supplements-for-dogs-with-cancer/
http://www.cancervetsfl.com/radiation-therapy-dogs-cats/
http://www.cancervetsfl.com/chemotherapy-dogs-cats/
https://www.caninecancer.com/surgery/
https://www.k9-medibles.com/cbd-oil-for-dogs-with-cancer/
https://www.thesprucepets.com/heart-disease-in-dogs-3384856
https://www.lifewithdogs.tv/2012/03/top-ten-signs-of-heart-disease-in-dogs/
https://www.healthline.com/health/9-warning-signs-dog-needs-veterinarian
https://www.365vet.co.uk/blog/common-causes-heart-disease-in-dogs/
http://caninekidneydisease.net/
https://www.vetinfo.com/canine-kidney-disease-treatment.html
http://www.vetstreet.com/our-pet-experts/how-to-say-goodbye
https://psychcentral.com/lib/the-5-stages-of-loss-and-grief/
https://www.petmd.com/dog/care/evr_dg_euthanasia_what_to_expect
https://www.thesprucepets.com/ways-to-remember-your-pet-4427802

Made in the USA
Las Vegas, NV
09 May 2024